GREAT REVIVALS

Great Revivals

God's Men and Their Message

Colin Whittaker

Collins
Marshall Pickering

William Collins Sons & Co. Ltd
London · Glasgow · Sydney · Auckland
Toronto · Johannesburg

First published in Great Britain in 1984 by
Marshall Pickering

This revised edition published in 1990

Marshall Pickering is an imprint of
Collins Religious Division,
part of the Collins Publishing Group
8 Grafton Street, London W1X 3LA

Printed and bound in Great Britain by
Cox & Wyman Ltd, Reading, Berks.

Dedication

To Edward England with thanks for first opening the door into books for me and countless others. With heartfelt appreciation for his unique contribution to Christian Publishing, and for his somehow always managing to combine a hard head with a soft heart.

Contents

Foreword

Many in the churches long for revival; some dread the thought of it. 'What is the point of revivals?' I once heard a theologian ask: 'they always come to an end!' The fact is that during spiritual revivals many thousands come to a saving knowledge of Jesus Christ and become inheritors of God's Kingdom. They are rescued from darkness and brought into light. Those who are bound for hell find new life in Jesus, can enjoy fellowship with God now and enjoy His heavenly glory eternally. That fact alone makes revivals worthwhile.

Any time of revival is a gift from God, and the fact that He gives such times is an indication that they are on His agenda. This book reviews some notable seasons of blessing and the fruit that has resulted from them. It makes stimulating reading and increases one's hunger to see such an outpouring of God's Spirit in our time.

This is a timely book, for many believe the Lord is preparing for a revival in Britain, perhaps the greatest move of evangelism this country has yet seen. Not that Colin Whittaker makes extravagant claims; but his enthusiasm for his subject is plain.

Although much of the book is a review of past blessing, Colin is keen to draw out certain principles that seem common to most, or all, revivals. Paramount among these is a centrality of prayer. Revivals begin as

God's response to the heart-cries of His people, not only praying for the lost, but facing their own need of spiritual revival.

Colin rightly draws out the distinction between *revival* of God's people and the subsequent *awakening* in the nation or area. It is when Christians are spiritually alive that they are able to be salt for the earth, light for the world, a city set on a hill that cannot be hidden.

Prevailing prayer can be costly. If we were to ask why the Church is not in a permanent state of revival, we would have to confess that the principle reason is that such times are costly. The Church seems to lapse into periods of sleepiness when its witness becomes largely ineffective and the nation consequently drifts further away from God. This demonstrates that revival is necessary.

The cost is not only in prayer. It is the fervent prayers of the righteous that avail much before God. During times of revival there is a real concern among Christians for righteousness and holiness; to be more Christ-like.

Only if Christians are living in righteousness will they have an effective witness into a nation where there is much unrighteousness. Only if they are living in love, joy and peace themselves can they bring hope into what is largely a hopeless society. It is only when they put the claims of the Gospel above all other considerations, seeking first the Kingdom of God and His righteousness, that they find God meeting with them in their needs and ready to bless others through them.

This is not to say that men can contrive revivals, nor can they ever deserve them. They can only seek God for such times of blessing while being prepared to let the work begin in their own hearts and lives. So there is little point in praying for revivals unless we are prepared for God to meet with us, to bring our lives into closer conformity with His will and purpose.

God works out His purpose through men. It is inevitable that in any revival and subsequent awakening certain personalities come to the fore. But the message of this book is clear: during any such time of blessing it is the Lord Jesus Christ Himself who is central and the men God uses greatly are those who proclaim and honour Him.

It is my prayer that God will use this book to stir your heart towards a greater desire for revival in your own life and in the Church as a whole, so that we might confidently believe that we shall see a great awakening in this land. As you read these pages let the Holy Spirit stir your heart to believe that the things seen in former times will be seen again, but in an even more glorious way. For if there is any feature that marks the present day awakening already happening in many lands, it is the fact that mighty signs and wonders are attending the preaching of the Gospel of the Kingdom of God. He is in the business of turning nations back to Himself, and it is the prayer of many that His Spirit will be poured out afresh on this land with sovereign power.

COLIN URQUHART

Revival

The growing interest in Revival has resulted in many trusted servants of God sharing their thoughts on this vital subject. Prayer gatherings for Revival have proliferated. The vast 'Prayer for Revival' meetings under the leadership of Bob Dunnett, Graham Kendrick, and Ian Cuthbert, in the National Exhibition Centre, Birmingham, have attracted crowds of twelve thousand and more. Leading magazines such as *Renewal*, *Restoration*, and *Redemption* have majored on the topic. Here is a selection of vital observations on the subject, most of them recent, all of them relevant, along with some great scriptures which have stirred intercessors throughout the centuries.

'For thus saith the high and lofty One that inhabiteth eternity, whose name is Holy; I dwell in the high and holy place, with him also that is of a contrite and humble spirit, to revive the spirit of the humble, and to revive the heart of the contrite ones.' Isaiah 57:15

'Revival is not normally something which comes upon the church of God unless people somewhere are moving with the vision of it.' The Rev. Bob Dunnett, Vice-Principal of the Birmingham Bible Institute and Chairman of Prayer for Revival.

'There is up-to-date evidence that God is still pouring out his Spirit in revival power, whatever theories there may be to the contrary. In addition, and more importantly, this evidence helps us to catch something of the spirit and atmosphere of revival.' Arthur Wallis (from an article found on his word processor by his wife Eileen shortly after he had gone to be with the Lord).

'The history of revivals, both ancient and more recent, clearly indicates one overriding factor common to all of them – prayer. Nothing was accomplished of any significance except that the people of God first got serious about the matter of seeking God.' Floyd McClung (Head of YWAM in Europe).

'I have always understood revival as a sovereign act of God which begins in the church, leading men and women to a conviction of their sinfulness and a desire for repentance and cleansing. This results in a total commitment to Jesus Christ as Lord and Saviour. In other words, through the fire of his Holy Spirit, God restores his deep-frozen people to life. Alive with a burning love for Jesus, we then bring non-Christians to a place where they too can be set on fire by the Spirit and the process is repeated.' Charles Whitehead, successful businessman who is actively involved in Renewal circles on the National Service Committee for Catholic Renewal.

'Revival means God coming to a community face-to-face.' Brash Bonsall, Principal of the Birmingham Bible Institue, who has lived in the expectancy of the coming revival for over fifty years.

Characteristics of Holy Spirit Revival

'An intensified awareness of God, when even unbelievers and sceptics are compelled to acknowledge the presence of God.

'A jealous concern for the truth – revival and reform are always closely associated and any authentic work of the Spirit will lead to a rehabilitation of biblical doctrine.

'An absorbing concentration on prayer – if prayer plays a vital part in the promotion of revival it also remains a constant factor throughout its course; while its neglect is one of the major reasons for its decline.

'An exciting realisation of unity. In true revival all are one in Christ Jesus as the Spirit himself effects his own integration. Catholicity of spirit is the mark of revived Christianity. (Quotation from John Newton: "If a man loves Jesus, I will love him – whatever hard name he may be called by. His differing from me will not always prove him to be wrong, except I am infallible myself.")

'An augmented zeal in evangelism. Revival rekindles what our forefathers called "the passion for souls". It stimulates zeal to win others for Christ and supplies evangelism with a cutting edge because the priesthood of all believers is no longer regarded merely as a privilege: it is seen as a responsibility.' Dr D. A. Skevington-Wood, former Principal of Cliff College, speaking at the Evangelists' Conference.

'The last two years have seen in almost every nation of the world the sad stories of men of God who have fallen into sin. It has been amazing that God has been exposing the failures of Christian leaders in recent days like we have never seen before. Is this just a coincidence, or have we been going through a cleansing time prior to the ingathering? Students of Bible prophecy believe that there are three indicators of an ingathering. Firstly, there is a warning of the prophet who rises up and speaks out against the sins of the church. It is God's endeavour for His church to get right with Him so that judgement is avoided. If there is a failure to respond, then He exposes and starts cleansing His church. During this time there are periods of repentance, in which hidden sins are brought to the light, so that God may have a holy church in preparing for the great ingathering.

'As one studies revival, these three principles have always been in practice and over the last few years we have seen the fulfilment of two. There have been men of God rising up around the world, warning the church to put its house in order. Books have been written that have sold in the realm of hundreds and thousands. Powerful speakers have sent tape-recordings around the world saying that God is not pleased with the laxity and coldness of His church and that He wants them to repent. What followed was a cleansing period, and now we must prepare for the great ingathering of the Harvest.

'I believe that so great will be God's power that miracles will be commonplace, that multitudes of people will be healed, blind eyes will be opened, the lame will walk, many will be delivered of evil spirits and above all, millions will be born again and baptised in the Holy Spirit during this amazing time of God's outpouring.' Dr Andrew Evans, General Superintendent of Assemblies of God in Australia and senior minister at Paradise Assembly in Adelaide.

'Is revival a work of God, as Jonathan Edwards insisted, or a work of man, as C. G. Finney proposed? The biblical answer is clear: "Will you not revive us again?" cried the Psalmist; "Revive your work, O Lord!" requested the prophet; and both petitions were addressed to God. Nowhere in Scripture is any suggestion of plan or programme for self-revival. Neither denomination nor organisation, nor pastor nor evangelist, can organise an outpouring of the Holy Spirit.' Dr J. Edwin Orr (1912–1987), Historian of Revival.

'When we get excited about the signs and wonders that God is doing among us, let us remember the purpose behind them. We preach Christ the power of God and the wisdom of God. We point only to the Cross. And we share the Cross by dying ourselves to the flesh.' Jackie Pullinger.

'The Old and New Testaments are bristling with promises indicating God's willingness to send revival to those who trust him and obey the conditions he lays down. While Revival is a sovereign act of God, he makes it clear that if we do our part he will do his. Acts 3:19 says, "Repent therefore and turn again, that your sins may be blotted out, that times of refreshing may come from the presence of the Lord.'' A repentant, cleansed and refreshed church will turn again to service and be sent out to a needy world. I believe Revival is on the way. I believe the choice is ours – the fire of revival or the freezer of apathy?' John Noble, Leader of Team Spirit, based in Romford, Essex.

'The 70s was a decade of renewal; the 80s a decade of evangelism. The 90s will be a decade of revival. There has been a growing expectation that we shall see a sovereign move of God's Spirit in revival power. It is easy for people to become excited about revival and to engage in wishful thinking. But I believe the prophetic word of the Lord is that we shall move into a revival situation in the near future.' Colin Urquhart, Leader of Kingdom Faith Ministries based at Roffey Place in West Sussex.

'The ultimate purpose of revival is to change people and society.

'I believe what we have come to call "the Charismatic Renewal" is a revival. David Barrett has recently published figures which would indicate this. In 1970 there were 3.79 million charismatics in the world; five years later there were 16.86 million; by 1985 the number had risen to 97.50 million. By 1988 it was about 123 million. In the same period Pentecostals have grown from 64 million to 176 million worldwide. All this has taken place in the teeth of strong opposition.

'Revivals are not to be measured like earthquakes on a kind of Richter scale of scalps. But the size and scope of this move of God marks it out as the largest in the whole of church history. Moreover it continues to grow at the rate of 19 million a year or 54,000 a day.

'But it is not only its size which makes it eligible to be counted as one of the great revivals of all time. It also came as a surprise. No one was expecting it. Still today the leaders of the great churches do not take it seriously. Some despise it, for its leaders are "nobodies". God has chosen the foolish things of this world, and shown what he can do with weak human material, and it still puzzles those who cannot accept it. Some wish it would just go away.

'If I am right, we should be praying that the Renewal will fulfil the purpose for which it was sent – not to entertain and comfort God's people but to reach out to the world and bring the harvest in. We should be looking, in other words, for the fruit of revival.' Canon Michael Harper, International Executive Director of SOMA (Sharing of Ministries Abroad), an Anglican mission agency dedicated to fostering renewal in the Holy Spirit worldwide.

Here is the table of figures of the Major Religions in 1989 as released at *Lausanne II* – the gathering of Evangelical Christian leaders of the world – in Manila, 11–20 July, 1989.

'IF MY PEOPLE, WHICH ARE CALLED BY MY NAME, SHALL HUMBLE THEMSELVES, AND PRAY, AND SEEK MY FACE, AND TURN FROM THEIR WICKED WAYS: THEN WILL I HEAR FROM HEAVEN, AND WILL FORGIVE THEIR SIN, AND WILL HEAL THEIR LAND.'

THE LORD GOD ALMIGHTY (II Chronicles 7:14)

MAJOR RELIGIONS IN 1989
from David Barrett's
WORLD CHRISTIAN ENCYCLOPEDIA
(London: Oxford University Press)

World Population	5,163 million

of WORLD RELIGIONS

Christian	1,722 million
Muslim	908 million
Hindu	690 million
Buddhist	320 million
Jewish	18 million

of CHRISTIANS

Roman Catholics	944 million
Protestant	363 million
Eastern Orthodox	175 million
Marginal Christians	178 million

of PROTESTANTS

Denominational Pentecostals	185,544,360
Anglicans	52,376,800
Baptists	52,093,494
Lutherans	45,503,675
Presbyterians	45,215,569
Methodists	32,970,691

of PENTECOSTALS

Denominational Pentecostals	185 million
Protestant Charismatics	18 million
Catholic Charismatics	30 million
Chinese Pentecostal Charismatics	38 million
Mainline Post-charismatics	70 million
Mainline Third-Wavers	28 million
Total World %	17.55%
World Total	352,000,000

1

The Fourth 'R'

Dr. Martin Lloyd-Jones in his masterly book *Preaching and Preachers* stated 'I know of nothing, in my own experience, that has been more exhilarating and helpful, and that acted more frequently as a tonic to me, than the history of Revivals. Church history, and especially the history of Revivals is one of the best antidotes to a preacher's discouragement and depression in the time we are living in.' This book is simply a dose of such tonic as the Doctor prescribed.

Revival has been described as the fourth R; the three R's being Reformation (doctrine), Renewal (dynamics), and Restoration (direction); but Revival is God taking the field.

Revivals are not confined to any particular part of Church history; they are a recurring phenomenon throughout the centuries and in every part of the world. As E. J. Poole-Connor observed, 'There have been many such visitations of grace, both in Britain and abroad. Their most obvious explanation is that they are supernatural in character and wrought by the Spirit of God.' (*Evangelicalism in England*) All kinds of people have been used of God in revival; learned and unlearned, emotional and phlegmatic. All types, temperaments and nationalities have been the subjects of revival.

D. M. Panton aptly described revival as 'the inrush of

the Spirit into a body that threatens to become a corpse'. When Methodism was threatening to settle down into a dead formality in the generation after the passing of John Wesley, then an inrush of the Spirit at the beginning of the 19th century produced the Primitive Methodist Revival. With it came a host of anointed characters such as John Benton, whose preaching produced the same kind of effects as Peter's on the Day of Pentecost when the hearers were pierced in their hearts. John Benton (labelled like Peter an 'unlearned and ignorant man') was once criticised for his lack of grammar. Benton went quietly on his way until one Good Friday his unfortunate critic was present and saw rugged miners falling down under conviction after Benton had preached on Christ's words on the cross, 'It is finished'. He could not resist observing to his critic 'This is grammar!' Yes, and that is the fourth R; that is Revival! Conviction of sin is a hall-mark of genuine revival. Edwin Orr says of Acts 2:37 which describes the effects of Peter's preaching that the hearers were 'pricked, pierced, stabbed, stung, stunned, smitten – these are the synonyms of a rare verb which Homer used to signify being drummed to earth.'

A character in direct contrast to John Benton was the Rev. John Livingstone, a very able Reformed minister who lived at the beginning of the 17th century. The story of the revival at Shotts was one that Dr. Martin Lloyd-Jones acknowledged as one of his particular favourites. Livingstone had had to flee to Northern Ireland for a time because of persecution; while there he had some experiences of revival. In 1630 he was back in Scotland and was at a great Communion season at Kirk O'Shotts, a place about mid-way between Edinburgh and Glasgow. These Communion seasons lasted several days and were characterised by much preaching. On this occasion the leaders felt from the outset that there was something special about the gathering, and instead of finishing on the Sunday they decided to have an extra service on the

Monday and asked John Livingstone to preach.

He was overwhelmed at the responsibility, being a humble and modest man, and consequently he spent most of the night prior to June 21st, 1630, in prayer. Many of the people were praying also. But Livingstone was in a great agony of soul and could find no peace until the early hours of Monday morning when God gave him a message and an assurance that his preaching would be attended with great power. The service took place in the open air and after he had been preaching for over an hour a few drops of rain disconcerted the people. Livingstone asked them if they had any shelter from the storm of God's wrath and went on for another hour, exhorting and warning his hearers. His text was Ezekiel 36:25–26, (A new heart also will I give you . . .). He himself said, 'I had such liberty and melting of heart as I never had the like in public all my life.' The Spirit of God so moved upon the great congregation that many were smitten to the ground under great conviction. As a result of that one sermon, some 500 people were converted and added to the churches in the area. That is the fourth R; that is Revival! It is an outpouring of the Spirit of God as on the Day of Pentecost.

In 1739 George Whitefield was challenged to try and convert the colliers of Kingswood, Bristol. They were notorious for their drunkenness and degradation. As the churches had closed their doors to him, Whitefield wrote, '. . . Finding that the pulpits are denied me, and the poor colliers are ready to perish for lack of knowledge, I went to them and preached to upwards of two hundred. Blessed be God that the ice is now broken and I have now taken to the field.'

Next day when he returned to preach to them he found their numbers had increased to several thousand. They filled the fields, the paths, the roads; they clambered on walls and climbed into trees. A great silence came over them as Whitefield lifted his marvellous voice so that they were all able to hear. As he looked down on this vast crowd he first discovered that they were being deeply affected when he saw (to use his own words), 'the white gutters made by their tears, which plentifully fell down their black cheeks . . . Hundreds and hundreds of them were soon brought under deep conviction, which happily ended in a sound and thorough conversion.' That is the fourth R; that is Revival! It is the demonstration of the Spirit of God in power.

Revival sometimes comes when least expected. The saintly David Brainerd toiled day and night among the Red Indians of North America: he spent days praying and fasting but with little effect. Then on August 8th, 1745, the break came. He wrote in his journal, 'It is remarkable that God began this work among the Indians at a time when I had the least hope and, to my apprehension, the least rational prospect of seeing a work of grace propagated among them. My hopes respecting the conversion of the Indians were perhaps never reduced to so low an ebb as at this time. Yet this was the very season in which God saw fit to begin his glorious work.' In his journal for that day he wrote, 'In the afternoon I preached to the Indians upon Luke 15:16–23. There was much visible concern among them while I was discoursing publicly; but afterwards, when I spoke to one and another more particularly, whom I perceived under much concern, the power of God seemed to descend upon the assembly 'like a mighty rushing wind', and with an astonishing energy bore down all before it.

'I stood amazed at the influence which seized the audience almost universally, and could compare it to nothing more aptly than the irresistible force of a mighty torrent. All ages were bowed down with concern. The most stubborn hearts were now obliged to bow. They were almost universally praying and crying for mercy and numbers could neither go nor stand.'

Brainerd was never fluent in the Indian dialects and on one occasion had to preach through a drunken interpreter; yet scores were converted as the Spirit of God moved upon them like a rushing mighty wind. That is the fourth R; that is Revival! It is supernatural; it is the Spirit of God at work.

Revival happenings such as these are not confined to the post-Reformation era; far from it. The brave Waldenses, who provided more than their quota of martyrs, experienced a revival in the 12th century which resulted in great evangelistic activity especially in Southern France and Northern Italy, but which also reached Bohemia. It was estimated that there were 80,000 true believers in Bohemia in 1315. This remarkable revival prepared the way for the move of God under John Huss. In the time of Wycliffe (1320–84), revival phenomena occurred in many parts of Britain through the preaching of the Lollards.

Going further back to the post-apostolic era of the early Church, the story is the same. Charles Spurgeon, preaching on revival in the time of the 1859 revival, said, 'Have you never heard of the mighty things which God did by preachers then? Has it not been told you concerning Chrysostom (344–407 AD), the golden-mouthed, who, whenever he preached, the church was thronged with attentive hearers; and there, standing and lifting up holy hands, he spoke with a majesty unparalleled; the word of God in truth and righteousness; the people listening, hanging forward to catch every word, and anon breaking the silence with the clapping of their hands and the stamping of their feet; then silent again for a while, spell-bound by the mighty orator; and anon carried away with enthusiasm, springing to their feet, clapping their hands and shouting for joy again? Numberless were the conversions in his day; God was exceedingly magnified, for sinners were abundantly saved.'

Can we expect revival in our day? Let Spurgeon answer that familiar question from the same sermon which he preached on July 17th, 1859. 'When people hear about what God used to do, one of the things they say is: "Oh, that was a long time ago." I thought it was God that did it. Has God changed? Is He not an immutable God? Does not that furnish an argument to prove what God has done at one time He can do at another? Nay, I think I may push it a little further, and say what He has done once, is a prophecy of what He intends to do again. Whatever God had done in the way of converting sinners is to be looked upon as a precedent. Let us take the blame of it ourselves, and with earnestness seek that God would restore to us the faith of the men of old, that we may richly enjoy His grace as in the days of old.'

The fact is that revivals have been taking place in many parts of the world throughout this century, in countries such as Brazil, Indonesia, Borneo and Korea. Korea especially has become a challenge and an object lesson to the whole of Christendom. It is only one hundred years since the first missionaries brought the gospel to Korea, but in spite of suffering, persecution and war, Korea has been enjoying successive revivals. In planning an International Prayer Assembly to celebrate the centennial of the introduction of Christianity in Korea in 1984, Dr. Ben Jennings, the conference co-ordinator said, 'Many of us believe a great worldwide revival is imminent . . . this Prayer Assembly could well be the spark to ignite and accelerate the flame of global spiritual awakening.'

General William Booth was quick to realise at the time of the Ulster Revival of 1859 that the record of what the Holy Spirit had done in the past was the secret of His working in the present. It is imperative to learn all we can from the records of past revivals in order to be prepared for the revival which many key Christian leaders of many denominations believe 'is at hand'.

Before proceeding it should be made clear what the

writer understands by the word 'revival'. Money is not the only thing that suffers devaluation: precious words can also be affected until they hold as little worth as the old German mark, when a million marks would scarcely buy a loaf of bread. Such is this word 'revival'. Some (especially in America) have used it as a synonym for an evangelistic crusade. This probably came about because of the rare occasions when evangelistic campaigns turned into times of revival visitations, but that was the exception rather than the rule.

By revival we mean those special seasons of divine visitation when God the Holy Ghost quickens and stirs the slumbering Church of God. Believers are set ablaze for Christ and the power of God is so manifest in prevailing prayer and anointed preaching of the gospel that the most hardened and sceptical unbelievers are brought under great conviction of sin, leading in turn to genuine repentance and saving faith in the Lord Jesus Christ, through His death on the cross and resurrection.

Edwin Orr says, 'The logic of words suggests "revival" for revitalizing of a body of Christian believers, and "awakening" for the stirring of interest in the Christian faith in the related community of nominal Christians or unbelievers.' The Oxford Association for Research in Revival has adopted 'revival' for believers, and 'awakening' for community.

The Acts of the Apostles is the pattern by which all revivals are judged. It is significant that it covers a period of approximately thirty-three and a half years, about the same period as the life of the Son of God on earth. In the short space of one generation the gospel spread from Jerusalem to Rome. As it is the only unfinished book in the Bible, obviously by design, its purpose seems to be to remind the Church that God's purpose is that the living Christ shall be presented to each generation in the power of the Spirit.

After Peter had preached in Jerusalem on the Day of

Pentecost we read, 'When the people heard this, they were cut to the heart and said to Peter and the other apostles, "Brothers, what shall we do?" Peter replied, "Repent and be baptised, every one of you, in the name of Jesus Christ so that your sins may be forgiven. And you will receive the gift of the Holy Spirit. The promise is for you and your children and for all who are far off – for all whom the Lord our God will call." With many other words he warned them; and he pleaded with them, "Save yourselves from this corrupt generation." Those who accepted his message were baptised, and about three thousand were added to their number that day.' (Acts 2:37–41 NIV)

That is the fourth R; that is Revival.

2

1734 – New England

The revival in New England was one of the most significant of the 18th Century. Out of a population of 250,000 at least 50,000 were added to the Church. This very high proportion of new converts 'revolutionised the religious and moral character of the area and had a profound effect on the entire country'.

What is so encouraging is that this outpouring of God's Spirit came when it was most sorely needed. The passion and fervour of the Pilgrim Fathers was sadly lacking in the thirteen colonies of their descendants a century after those pioneer days. One of the paramount causes of decline (as Joseph Tracey explains in his fine work *The Great Awakening*) was the admission of unconverted people into church membership. The decision of the Synod of 1662 hastened the decline. Soon there were unconverted ministers as well as unconverted communicants.

'God's methods are men', and the man in this case was Jonathan Edwards. He was born on October 5th, 1703, the only son of Timothy Edwards, pastor in East Windsor, Connecticut, a frontier village. Jonathan, a humble and deeply spiritual person, was widely recognised as one of the greatest theologians in American history. He studied at Yale College and received his M.A. in 1723; in May, 1724, he became tutor at the College. His grandfather, Solomon Stoddard, was one of the leading ministers of the period and built up a great reputation in his fifty-seven years in the one church from 1672 to 1729. His influence had made Northampton the most important pulpit in New England – outside of Boston, and his long ministry was punctuated with special times of blessing and many conversions.

In 1727 Jonathan Edwards was ordained associate pastor to his grandfather at Northampton. The following year he married Sarah Pierrepont of New Haven. They enjoyed thirty happy years together and had twelve children.

It was no small honour for one so young to be called to succeed the revered Solomon Stoddard ('the unofficial Pope of the Connecticut valley'). Jonathan proved himself more than equal to the task, however, both in mind and, even more importantly, in heart. Ever since his conversion (which he himself places in the second year of his graduate studies when he was seventeen), he realised that the heart came first, and the test of religious truth was an inward sense. 'A sense of the heart', was a favourite phrase throughout his ministry; not mere intellectual belief, not just an acceptance of 'a form of words', but a definite witness within. As a child he was deeply religious, but only at seventeen years did he begin to understand the new birth and justification by faith. He describes it in his famous 'Personal Narrative'. As he was reading the scripture, 'Now unto the King eternal, immortal, invisible, the only wise God, be honour and glory for ever and ever, Amen' (I Tim. 1:17), he says, 'There came into my soul, and was as it were diffused through it, a sense of the glory of the Divine Being; a new sense quite different from anything I ever experienced before. From about that time I began to have new ideas of Christ, and the work of redemption, and the glorious way of salvation by Him. And my mind was greatly engaged to spend my time in reading and meditating on Christ, on the beauty and excellency of His person, and the lovely way of salvation by free grace in Him. The sense I had of divine things would often of a sudden kindle up, as it were, a sweet burning in my heart; an ardour of soul, that I know not how to express.'

That experience remained with him; it was the foundation of his preaching power and his inner strength. The conversion of chosen leaders is often the prelude to the revival God is planning. Jonathan Edwards, like Paul, was undoubtedly a chosen vessel.

Two years after coming to Northampton, his grandfather died leaving Edwards the sole occupant of the pulpit. The last few years of Solomon Stoddard's ministry had been a time of decline (possibly due to his age) and the spiritual life of the church and the moral life of the town suffered accordingly.

Edwards was concerned at the state of things and totally committed himself to the ministry of the Word and the care of his flock. He strongly disagreed with the 'Halfway Covenant' of 1662 which had ultimately resulted in compromises over church membership. Jonathan insisted upon conversion as a condition for acceptance into church membership.

As Joseph Tracy says in *The Great Awakening*, 'The New England Puritans believed that when a man is "born again" a change is wrought in him, of which it is possible for him and others to find evidence; that the regenerate differ from the unregenerate by the possession of some substantial good qualities, which must show themselves in thought, feeling and conduct, and they felt bound to treat all as unregenerate in whom, on examination, no evidence of Christian piety could be found.'

In 1734 Edwards preached a powerful series of sermons on 'Justification by faith alone'. Suddenly the Spirit of God began to work in power amongst them. It surprised even those who had prayed for it. Edwards described what happened, 'It was in the latter part of December that the Spirit of God began extraordinarily and wonderfully to work amongst us. Very suddenly, one after another, five or six persons were to all appearances savingly converted. Some of them were wrought upon in a very remarkable manner. A great and earnest concern about the great things of religion and the eternal world became universal in all parts of the town, among all classes and all ages. The work of conversion was carried on in a most astonishing manner and increased more and more; souls did come as it were by flocks to Jesus Christ. From day to day, for many months together, might be seen evident instances of sinners brought out of darkness into marvellous light. This work of God as it was carried on and the number of true saints multiplied, soon made a glorious alteration in the town so that in the spring and summer following (1735), the town seemed to be full of the presence of God.'

As Arthur Skevington Wood comments, 'The extent of this movement in a small town of not more than a couple of hundred families is nothing short of miraculous. Edwards set down the incredible statistics. In the months of March and April 1735, when the work of God was at its peak, he estimated the number of attested conversions to have been at least four a day or nearly thirty a week. Over three hundred came to Christ in the space of six months, with an equal proportion of men and women.' (*The Inextinguishable Blaze*.) This is significant because his grandfather (Solomon Stoddard) had told Edwards that during his ministry many more women were converted than men.

Jonathan Edwards counselled his converts personally and thoroughly. He did all within his power to ensure that each seeker passed through a true repentance into the experience of the new birth. The parsonage was thronged with enquirers and on one Sunday morning one hundred new converts were received into membership.

From several contemporary writers it seems that Jonathan Edwards was a quiet preacher. In the early part of his ministry he used a full manuscript when preaching and spoke quietly but clearly without any gestures. He was tall but of spare build, with piercing eyes. He spoke and looked as if in the presence of God, and could hold the attention of his hearers with his inspired and penetrating words. However, during the months when the revival was at its height, numbers of his hearers were under such conviction and in such distress that they cried out and wept loudly. Some were so overcome that they fell down, others seemed to faint. Visions and dreams and other such manifestations occurred during the years of the 'Great Awakening'. Many of these manifestations were genuine and Edwards was reluctant to interfere when he found that many of those affected proved to be lastingly changed. Some excesses occurred and others less wise and mature than Edwards made too much of them and concentrated on the physical phenomena rather than on the spiritual realities.

That this was a work of the Spirit of God and not mere human emotion and excitement was proved by the fact that people of all ages were affected, not merely the young and impressionable. Edwards, in his own narrative of the revival, rejoices in the conversion of many middle aged and elderly people. He wrote, 'It has been heretofore rarely heard of that any were converted past middle age; but now I suppose there were upwards of fifty persons converted in this town above forty years of age; more than twenty of them above fifty; and ten of them above sixty; and two of them above seventy years of age.' During these days of revival, Edwards said that 'there was as much done in a day or two as at ordinary times is done in a year.' Visitors who came into the town on business or to stay with friends were nearly all affected by the wonderful atmosphere. Their consciences soon began to trouble them, conviction was followed by conversion and (wrote Edwards), 'they went home rejoicing; till at length the same work began to appear and prevail in several other towns in the county.' Some, however, scoffed and ridiculed and compared the conversion to 'certain distempers'. Nevertheless the work spread and increased rapidly, being carried to many other towns and villages in New Hampshire and over into Connecticut.

In Northampton the revival peaked in 1735 and then subsided somewhat, one very good reason being (as Joseph Tracy suggests in *The Great Awakening*) that virtually the whole population of the town had been affected and there were no longer any 'new subjects to be found'. One tragic incident also adversely affected things for a time. One Lord's Day morning, Joseph Hawley, an uncle of Jonathan Edwards and one of the chief men of the town, cut his throat and died instantly. The town was aghast, and took some time to recover from this sad suicide.

The news of the revival brought letters from far and wide requesting information and Edwards answered them as time allowed. His letter to Benjamin Colman of Boston was published by him and forwarded to London, which led to requests for more details. The result was a longer account which was published in London under the title of *A Faithful Narrative of the surprising Work of God in the Conversion of Many Hundred Souls in Northampton and the Neighbouring Towns and Villages*. It appeared in 1737 and subsequently was published in England with an introduction by Isaac Watts and John Guyse. In the Preface they wrote, 'Never did we hear or read, since the first ages of Christianity, any event of this kind so surprising as the present narrative.' It was widely read in Britain and played an important part in stirring Christians to see the need and possibility of revival. Indeed it was in this way that the revival in Northampton in 1735 was the 'initial spark of the Evangelical Revival in Great Britain'. It gave many ministers new views of what can happen in times of revival, and stirred them to seek

God for a similar visitation. A century later, Joseph Tracy in his carefully researched and historic work *The Great Awakening* said that Jonathan Edward's narrative 'should be attentively studied by everyone whose duty it is to understand the workings of the human mind under the convicting and converting influences of the Spirit of God'.

S. E. Dwight in his biography of Edwards pointed out that, 'For a long period, revivals had been largely unknown in Europe. The church had ceased to expect them. The story of the work of grace at Northampton produced a general conviction in the minds of Christians, that the preaching of the gospel might be attended with the same effects as in apostolic times.' It seems that the telling of a revival often stimulates the faith of others and leads to further revivals. Later, John Wesley republished Edward's account for his followers to believe for similar results.

In 1740 the fires of revival throughout New England were rekindled in an even greater way by the visit of George Whitefield. 'With his coming the awakening, which had started in 1734, and then had partially subsided, now burst again into full flame.' (F. W. Hoffman.)

Whitefield first visited New England in September 1740, and preached at Newport, Rhode Island with great power. It was the prelude to the greatest single evangelistic tour in New England's history and the most remarkable and widespread quickening the American colonies had known. Whitefield's fame had preceded him and his arrival was anticipated with great eagerness which was not disappointed. The Spirit of God moved through his preaching and the work spread throughout the colonies like a prairie fire.

Vast crowds of many thousands thronged to hear the anointed Whitefield. His fiery and dramatic eloquence, his passion, his power gripped the people. Whitefield rejoiced, 'O how the Word did run. It rejoiced my heart

29

to see such numbers greatly affected . . . many wept exceedingly.' Pastors declared that they had more enquirers within a month than they had had previously throughout the whole of their ministry.

What a meeting that was when for the first time these two great men of God – Whitefield and Edwards – came together at Northampton. Whitefield was most impressed with Jonathan Edwards and said he had seen no-one like him in all New England. Edwards in turn wept unashamedly as Whitefield preached in his church at Northampton. The visit stirred the embers into flame again and the work continued for two glorious years. Whitefield's tour of New England covered only six weeks but the revival flourished long afterwards. The Awakening of 1734 and 1735 had been localised in the area around Northampton but this revival was much more wide-spread. In January 1742, Edwards was able to write, 'By what I can understand, the work of God is greater at this day in the land than it has been at any time.' The impact of Whitefield's visit must never be minimised but over the years it was Edwards who proved to be its true leader.

During the 1740's Edwards travelled long distances on horseback, preaching and exercising a revival ministry in districts far from Northampton. But he was not alone in the work and many other able ministers aided him in those great years.

The only thing many people know about Jonathan Edwards is the famous incident when he preached his sermon 'Sinners in the hands of an angry God,' and which caused some to label him as a 'terrorist preacher'. For the record it should be said that he had already preached this same sermon in his own pulpit without unusual effect. Of the 568 sermons he left behind, most of them cover positive biblical themes such as the glory of salvation, the peace that Christ gives, the reality of spiritual light, the gentleness of Jesus, and comfort in the thought of heaven. This one on the wrath of God was an exception.

The impression it made on the congregation at Enfield, on Sunday morning, July 8th, 1741, was also exceptional and remarkable. The town of Enfield had until then resisted the influence of the revival. His text was from Deut. 32:35 'Their foot shall slide in due time.' His theme was the fear of an eternity without salvation; of an angry God who would take vengeance on those who had lived without Him; of the uncertainty of life and the certainty of the eternal torment of sinners in hell.

He was a guest speaker on this occasion and unknown to the congregation at Enfield except by reputation, and at the beginning of the service the people were careless and indifferent. He stood to preach as usual with his tiny sermon booklet in his left hand; occasionally speaking extemporaneously, by way of illustration or enlargement, as he read what he had written. But as the sermon proceeded the Holy Spirit convicted them of sin, righteousness, and judgement. Suddenly they were overwhelmed and they felt their peril as never before. Strong men were gripped with the most awful fear of hell; some of them felt they were already slipping down into the fires of a lost eternity and they clung to the pillars of the meeting-house and cried aloud for mercy. So great was the crying at one point that the preacher's voice was drowned and he had to stop and ask for silence. The results were lasting and the revival had at last come to Enfield as to the rest of the colony.

Wherever Edwards preached in those years it seemed that his ministry prospered and was marvellously owned of God. Although Enfield was unique his preaching was followed constantly by remarkable results and scenes. Unfortunately, however, relations between pastor and people at Northampton were increasingly strained. There were several causes. The pastor's salary was a perennial cause of dispute in many churches and Northampton was no exception – even after the revival! The course of revival – like true love – seldoms runs smoothly. At the height of the money problem there was an incident over some of the members' children reading 'bad books'; Jonathan Edwards made a public issue of it and antagonised some of the leading families in the town, whose children were involved.

This was followed shortly after by the question of admitting non-members and uncommitted people to the Lord's Supper; Edwards made a great issue of it and would not back down. Opposition in the town was led by Joseph Hawley, the son of the man who had committed suicide during the 1735 revival, and he harboured his private grudge. Finally on June 22nd, 1750, Edward's church dismissed him. He was shocked but unshaken. He preached his farewell sermon without any bitterness and with great dignity.

In 1751 he became the pastor of the frontier church at Stockbridge, Massachusetts, and missionary to the Red Indian settlement there. He wrote some of his best-known works during his six years there as well as preaching and carrying out his other duties faithfully. On September 29th, 1757 he was invited to the presidency of the College of New Jersey (now Princeton). The town was in the throes of an epidemic; Edwards was inoculated on his arrival but he suffered a secondary infection and died on March 22nd, 1758.

At the height of the revival, Jonathan Edwards sent out his famous appeal for Christians of all lands to 'unite together to pray for a world-wide awakening and a return to primitive apostolic Christianity'. Towards the end of that same century a copy of his appeal fell into the hands of William Carey and stirred him to his depths. He gathered a group of believers to pray that God would 'do a new thing' in their midst. Eventually Carey republished Edwards' revival appeal with far reaching results. In the nineteenth century the manifesto stirred Charles Finney and became the basis of his famous revival lectures. As Skevington-Wood so rightly says, 'Both as a promoter and expositor of evangelical life Edwards stands in the forefront of the 18th Century Awakening. No survey can afford to neglect him. Few could do him justice.' (*The Inextinguishable Blaze*.)

3

1735 – Wales: Howell Harris and Daniel Rowlands

God's timing is always perfect. As we have seen, the revival in New England centred on Northampton and Jonathan Edwards, was at full spate in 1735. In Great Britain, in that same year, God was calling His chosen men and preparing them as instruments of revival in 'the old country'. 1735 marked the conversions of George Whitefield in England and Howell Harris in Wales. These two were to be mightily used in tremendous times of revival which would arouse the church and radically improve society.

Although John Wesley and George Whitefield are the two best known names of the 18th Century revival, they were not the only ones, neither were they the first. Wales, the Land of Revivals, was the scene and source of the initial quickening; although at the beginning of the eighteenth century things were at a low ebb there also. Following the restoration of Charles II, Wales had declined politically and spiritually. There was in fact a revival of the wrong sort – an upsurge of the occult and the renewed practice of divination and black magic.

Howell Harris was only too typical of the Welsh youth of his day. From the age of seventeen, when his father died, he 'broke out into the devil's service'. When he was a little older he lost interest in his work as a school-master and was more concerned with 'gambling at dice, drinking, love-making and improving his personal appearance'. At the age of twenty-one, (the same age at which Whitefield was converted) Howell Harris was moved and affected by a sermon by the vicar of Talgarth and he began to try to amend his ways. As he sought God he came under deep conviction. At the Whit Sunday Communion service God met with him; he looked to Christ and Him crucified; he believed and rejoiced. He testified, 'I went home leaping for joy! I knew my sins were forgiven.'

From the first he was an evangelist; immediately he began to testify to his former companions. He gave himself to much prayer, and his biographer, Richard Bennett, said, 'In the secret place with his God, Harris was in his element'. Soon after his conversion, as he prayed alone for hours in the church tower of the village where he was then teaching, God met him in power. Dallimore adds, 'This was indeed a hallowed experience to Harris. It proved to be a mighty infilling of the Holy Spirit, empowering him for the ministry of incessant labours, violent opposition and spiritual victories which lay directly before him.'

Harris started by reading to the neighbours, then by visiting the sick. Next, he went from house to house in the locality and then in other villages. Crowds began to gather. He was sacked from teaching because of his preaching, so he became an itinerant evangelist. He sought ordination but was refused it: yet he had the 'ordination that really mattered – that of the pierced Hand' and the mantling of the Spirit's power.

His preaching was simple and direct. Like Bunyan he had 'a knack of adorning truth with an effective tale' and with striking figures of speech. People listened – even though sometimes he preached literally for hours – two, three, four and even six! He travelled throughout South

Wales preaching everywhere until the whole countryside was awakened. 'Hundreds were converted – among them some of the most notorious characters. Under the power of the Holy Spirit, hearts were broken and it was not uncommon for people to come under such conviction that they would cry out aloud to God for mercy while he preached.'

Like Wesley, Harris had exceptional gifts for organisation and he gathered his converts into societies. He formed his first society in September 1736, and by 1739, according to Whitefield, there were nearly thirty. This was the beginning of Welsh Calvinistic Methodism and it took place nearly two years before the Wesleys were converted.

In 1739 Whitefield crossed into Wales to meet Harris with whom he had been corresponding for some time. These two young men – still only twenty-four years old – were kindred spirits. They were white-hot evangelists calling all men to salvation; yet as Poole-Connor observes, 'both were believers in election and eternal security; and insisting on the necessity for a holy life to accompany an evangelical creed'.

What great days these two saw together! In Cardiff, Abergavenny, Pontypool, Chepstow, Harris preached in Welsh and Whitefield in English. They preached from horse-blocks, market crosses, walls of churchyards, tombstones and window-sills. Multitudes turned to Christ; it was revival! Dr. Thomas Rees called Harris 'the most successful preacher that ever ascended a pulpit or platform in Wales', and that is a stupendous claim in that land of preachers.

His brief visit to Wales over, Whitefield was soon bound for America once more, but Harris concentrated his labours on his beloved Wales. It was needed because swearing, lying, drunkenness, fighting and gambling were the order of the day. Harris itinerated throughout the country denouncing these vices and abuses and consequently he had to face the resentment of the mobs and rabble on many occasions. 'More than once he was left for dead, and many of his escapes were miraculous', says Joseph Ritson in *The Romance of Nonconformity*. He was beaten, stoned and trampled on. 'A companion was killed, his helpers seized by the press-gang, the clothes torn from the backs of his hearers.' Nevertheless he bravely persisted; he learned the secret of addressing great crowds and within half a dozen years he had roused Wales. A revival was set in progress which virtually ended the cruel sports and the promiscuous festivals of the time.

Daniel Rowlands' story is very different to that of Harris. He was ordained – but still unconverted. A keen athlete, he was far more interested in sport than in Christianity. But God also intervened in his life in a marvellous way.

The great Griffith Jones had gone to preach in the next village, at one of the three churches under Daniel Rowlands' charge, and it was only too apparent that the young curate was extremely sceptical. Griffith Jones has been justly called the morning star of the revival. Jones was then fifty-two years old and had carried with him a convincing spiritual authority ever since the call of God had come to him as a young man in a remarkable dream. He was then a shepherd and as he slept beside a hedge he claimed that 'an angel of the Lord lifted him up in a dream to show him all the joys of heaven and the torments of hell. He was then told that he was to be a chosen vessel to bear the name of Christ, a peculiar instrument for rescuing many souls.' He was not disobedient to the heavenly vision and the ensuing striking conversions, linked with his care for the poor and needy and his founding of many schools, confirmed his divine calling.

Griffith Jones was a great man of prayer and when he spotted the cynical expression on curate Daniel Rowlands' face, he paused to pray and sent an urgent plea to heaven for the conversion of this supercilious young man. More than that, Jones felt the touch of the Spirit inspiring him to pray that he might also become an instrument to turn many to righteousness. That prayer was abundantly answered, for in that very service Daniel Rowlands was convicted and converted.

Although his father was the rector of Llangeitho, Rowlands was abysmally ignorant of the gospel of Christ. He was born at Pant-y-beudy, near Llangeitho, in Cardiganshire, in 1713. He was ordained in 1733, two years after the death of his father. His elder brother John had succeeded his father in holding the three adjacent livings of Llangeitho, Llancwnlle and Llandewibrefi and Rowlands was ordained as curate to him.

Up to the time of his conversion, after preaching without any particular distinction each Sunday morning, Rowlands seems to have spent the rest of the Lord's day in sports and revels and drinking. The change in him and his preaching after his conversion was immediate and dramatic. He was now in the most dreadful earnest and he threw himself whole-heartedly into his ministry. He thundered out the wrath of God with such power and vehemence that his hearers were soon in deep distress and real fear of hell. His fame soon spread and crowds spilled over into the churchyards when he preached. Some came under such deep conviction that they lay down on the ground in the churchyard at Llancwnlle, and it was difficult for people to pass by without stumbling over their prostrate forms. However, in spite of this dramatic effect upon people, Daniel Rowlands was still without a clear understanding of the full gospel. This remarkable but far from satisfactory state of affairs continued for some four years. It was the 'Independent' and very successful preacher, Philip Pugh, who came to his aid. He took a great interest in young Rowlands at this critical period and pointed out to him that there was far too much Old Testament wrath and too little grace in his preaching. He said, 'If you go on preaching the law of Moses after this fashion you will kill half the people in the country, for you thunder out the curses of the law and preach it in such a terrible manner that no-one can stand before you.' Pugh went on to advise him 'Preach the gospel to the people and apply the balm of Gilead, the blood of Christ, to their spiritual wounds, and show the necessity of faith in the crucified Saviour.' Howell Harris also developed a friendship with Rowlands and from the help he received through these two great men, a new sweetness entered his preaching. From the age of thirty onwards he was established as a well-balanced preacher of the gospel. His sermons were now full of Christ and the Holy Spirit honoured them with the divine seals of success in bringing men and women to a saving faith in Christ.

William Williams writes: 'When he proclaimed free forgiveness through the sufferings and death of the Saviour of the world, sinners ready to perish felt that there was hope for them. In realising that hope, they rejoiced with joy unspeakable and full of glory, and great numbers expressed their ecstatic joy in shouts of praise.'

From then on for forty-seven glorious years he enjoyed almost continuous revival. Throughout those years he was seldom absent from Llangeitho on Sundays but even so he reached many thousands. On sacrament Sundays he often had between two thousand and two thousand five hundred communicants. People thought nothing of travelling fifty or sixty miles to hear him, and then they returned home singing the songs of Zion.

On weekdays he responded to invitations to preach in various parts of the Principality. One of his first invitations was to Ystradffin, some twenty miles away, over rough mountain roads. His ministry was owned of God by the conversion of thirty people that day. From then on he never hesitated to preach outside his own parish whenever there was opportunity, but he concentrated his ministry on Llangeitho, realising the necessity and importance of building up new converts in the faith. He combined the heart of an evangelist with that of a shepherd and, as the number of converts grew throughout the region, he realised the necessity of caring for them. With the aid of a few keen helpers – both lay and clerical – he established a regular system of societies, on the same lines as John Wesley's plan. Eventually this covered much of Wales and through these societies he kept in constant touch with the converts and kept them together. 'These societies', says Bishop J. C. Ryle, 'were all connected with one great Association, which met four times a year, and of which he was generally the moderator. The amount of his influence at these Association meetings may be measured by the fact that above one hundred ministers in the Principality regarded him as their spiritual father. From the first this Association seems to have been a most wisely organised and useful institution.'

Like Wesley and Whitefield he took to preaching frequently in the open-air, in fields, in market places, anywhere where crowds gathered. His first such effort came about through his burden to reach his former companions with the gospel. These sporting and pleasure-loving young men objected to his forthright sermons and refused to go to church. On Sundays they resorted to the hills above Llangeitho to amuse themselves with sports and games. Having failed to stop this practice he resolved to meet them on their own ground. He went to them and burst into the ring where a cock-fight was in progress, speaking to them fearlessly about their disgraceful conduct. Such was the effect of that sermon that no-one raised their voice against him and the gathering was permanently dissolved.

He had a powerful voice which enabled him to reach thousands in the open air without difficulty. He never lacked courage and he never allowed even the greatest dangers and the fiercest persecution and opposition to stop him. His life was frequently in danger. Once when he was preaching at Aberystwyth, a man swore that he would shoot him. He aimed his gun and actually pulled the trigger – but it failed to go off. On another occasion his enemies plotted to blow him up. They placed gunpowder under the place where he was to stand and preach and laid a trail of powder so that at the given time they could apply the match and blow up the preacher and congregation. Fortunately the plot was discovered in time and was foiled. At other times riotous mobs gathered and stones were thrown, drums beaten and every effort made to stop the preacher, but undeterred, Daniel Rowlands carried on with his great work.

As well as a great preacher, he was a great man of prayer. He often went to the top of the Aeron Hills to pour out his heart to God in fervent prayer for the salvation of the people in the region. It was said by those who knew him that he lived in the spirit of prayer and that this was a great secret of his success. On one occasion he was due to preach at a church which was on a hill top; he had to cross a valley in sight of the people who were waiting for him in the churchyard. They saw him descend into the valley out of their sight for a little while. They waited, expecting him to appear again as soon as he ascended from the valley, but the time came for the service to commence and he had still not appeared. Some went to search for him and they discovered him on his knees in a sheltered spot. He got up as soon as he saw them and went with them, expressing regret for the delay, but he added, 'I had a delightful opportunity below.' The sermon which followed was attended by extraordinary power.

The supreme secret of this man of God was his constant exaltation of Christ and Him crucified. His love and deep devotion to the Lord Jesus Christ often moved him to tears when preaching. On one never-to-be-forgotten occasion a most remarkable revival was sparked off at Llangeitho while Rowlands was reading the Anglican Litany. As he repeated the words, 'By thine agony and bloody sweat, good Lord, deliver us,' he did so with so much evident feeling that the whole congregation was immediately affected and was reduced to tears. Many began to weep loudly and an awakening of spiritual life commenced which extended throughout the neighbourhood.

All his life he remained poor, but he never complained and was content with his very simple lifestyle. He had opportunities to move to 'better livings' but preferred to remain in his beloved Llangeitho. His life was not without its trials but nothing moved him off course. It was a particularly sad day for him and for the episcopal church in Wales, when in 1763 the bishop revoked his license. Good Bishop Ryle comments, 'A more unhappy, ill-timed, blundering exercise of episcopal power than this, it is literally impossible to conceive! Here was a man of singular gifts and graces, who had no objection to anything in the Articles of Prayer-book, cast out of the Church of England for no other fault than excess of zeal. Rowlands was shut out of the Church of England and an immense number of his people all over Wales followed him.'

His friends and followers soon built him a large chapel nearby. He was not silenced even for a day and he continued on his way with undiminished power and blessing for twenty-seven more years, until his death at Llangeitho on October 16th, 1790, at the age of seventy-seven. He died peacefully, and towards the end he said, 'I have no more to state, by way of acceptance with God than I have always stated: I die as a poor sinner, depending fully and entirely on the merits of a crucified Saviour for my acceptance with God.' In his last hours, like John Wesley, he repeated frequently, 'God is with us.'

He was a man of great humility, always exalting his

42

Saviour and seeking His glory alone and never his own. He so preached the love of God in Christ that his hearers at times 'scarcely knew whether they were in heaven or on earth.' He was a most diligent student of the Word of God and his messages always combined gospel and sound doctrine for believers. It was the considered opinion of that most spiritual and shrewd judge of preachers, the Lady Huntingdon, that she thought Rowlands was second only to Whitefield as a preacher. His life and ministry prove that revival may continue with little or no abatement for many years. Bishop Ryle well says, 'Give us men like Rowlands with a like message and I have no fear that the Holy Ghost would grant us like results.'

4

England 1739: George Whitefield and John Wesley

'The year 1739 was one of astonishing expansion as the Evangelical Revival got under way', declares Arthur Skevington Wood in *The Inextinguishable Blaze*. The blessing commenced on New Year's day of 1739, of which Whitefield said, 'It was a Pentecostal season indeed.'

John and Charles Wesley and George Whitefield, with four others of the original Holy Club from their Oxford days, and some sixty others, gathered at Fetter Lane, London, in the evening to sing and pray. Whitefield wrote in his diary, 'Monday, 1st January, 1739. Had a love-feast with our brethren and spent the whole night in close prayer, psalms and thanksgiving. God supported me without sleep.' The hours flew by, until about three in the morning it seemed that the Day of Pentecost had come again. John Wesley in his journal recalled, 'The power of God came mightily upon us, insomuch that many fell to the ground. As soon as we were recovered a little from awe and amazement at the presence of His Majesty, we broke out with one voice, "We praise Thee, O God, we acknowledge Thee to be the Lord." '

On Friday of that same week, we read in Whitefield's diary, 'Held a conference at Islington, concerning several things of very great importance, with seven true ministers of Jesus Christ, despised Methodists, whom God has brought together from East, West, North and South.'

Though called Methodists, these seven were Anglican clergymen and had all, one by one, at different times experienced the greatest miracle of being born again through faith in Christ. They spent the day in fasting and prayer until 3 p.m. when, in the words of Whitefield, 'We parted with the full conviction that God was going to do great things among us.'

The situation in England certainly called for a special move of the Spirit of God, for things were in a desperate state. 'The whole population seemed to be given over to an orgy of drunkenness which made the very name of Englishmen to stink in the nostrils of other nations,' says Silvester Horne, in his *Popular History of the Free Churches*. We may think the permissive society of Britain in the latter part of the twentieth century has plumbed hitherto unreached depths, until we read the descriptions of Britain in the 1730's. 'Drunk for a penny, dead drunk for two-pence. Straw to lie on', was a common sign outside the pubs of that time.

The theatre was shockingly vulgar and depraved. Wesley referred to '. . . the obscenity of the stage – that sink of all corruption.' The literature of the period would even today be classed mostly as 'hard porn'. Polygamy, fornication, homosexuality were not considered sinful. Violence was rampant. 'Gangs of drunken ruffians paraded the streets and subjected women to nameless outrages, and defenceless men to abominable tortures. The constables shared the drunken habits of the time and were mainly corrupt.' Sport was cruel and brutal, such as bear and bull-baiting and cock-fighting. Pugilism was savage and murderous – and even women took part.

And what was the Church doing before 1739? For the most part sleeping. Bishop Ryle says, 'Both Anglicans and Non-conformists seemed at least agreed on one point

4 today! – 12/5/17

– and that was to let the devil alone and to do nothing for hearts and souls.'

But God was preparing His men and it is instructive to examine God's timetable for the years before 1739 and see how patiently He had been working in the lives of these men.

In 1732 Whitefield went to Oxford University as a servitor. (John Wesley had returned to Oxford in 1727 as a tutor). George Whitefield eventually linked up with Wesley's famed Holy Club, soon to be dubbed 'Methodists'. But all of these earnest and very religious men were still ignorant of the mysteries of the new birth.

1735 was the great year of discovery for Whitefield. After much heart-break and frustration; treading the devious paths of asceticism (he made himself very ill by severe fasting); legalistic religion, and so on, he discovered the secret of vital Christianity – the new birth and the free gift of salvation and forgiveness of sins through Christ alone. Immediately he joyfully wrote to his relative, 'I have found that there is such a thing as the new birth.'

Bishop Ryle claims, 'Of all the little band (of the Holy Club) none seem to have got hold so soon of clear views of Christ's gospel as he did. Whitefield majored on this great theme throughout his amazing ministry. He is said to have preached over a thousand times on the text, 'Ye must be born again' (John 3:7). Once when asked why he preached so often on that one text, he replied (with a twinkle in his squinty eye) "because YE MUST be born again!" Thirty-four years later he said, "I am now fifty-five years of age and I tell you that I am more convinced that the truth of the new birth is a revelation from God Himself, and that without it you can never be saved by Jesus Christ." In June 1736, Whitefield preached his first sermon in his home town of Gloucester. From the first, God's hand of power rested upon his preaching in a remarkable way. Some complained to the Bishop that

Whitefield had driven fifteen people mad; to which the Bishop replied, 'I hope their madness lasts until next Sunday.' Throughout the following year he preached at many public services and churches were crowded, especially in Bristol and London. His name was famous, whilst the Wesleys were still unknown.

Meanwhile, in 1735, John Wesley had become a missionary to the British Colony Georgia in America (forty-one years before America gained her independence). He had a most frustrating time there. He corresponded with Whitefield and finally urged him to join him in Georgia. At length Whitefield was persuaded and booked his passage to the New World. He sailed at the start of 1738 on the good ship *Whitaker*, and while crossing the Atlantic prayed, 'God give me a deep humility, a well-guided zeal, a burning love and a single eye and then let man and devils do their worst!' (from *George Whitefield* by Arnold Dallimore).

At this very time a frustrated Wesley had ended his short missionary career and decided to come home, bemoaning, 'I went to America to convert the Indians, but oh, wretched man that I am, who will convert me?' God did not keep him waiting much longer. John and Charles Wesley in a momentous double event by the Spirit of God, were led into the fulness of Christ within a few days of each other in May 1738. Charles was the first, and then on the evening of Wednesday, May 24th, John went very unwillingly to a meeting in Aldersgate Street, where someone was reading Luther's preface to the Epistle to the Romans. John Wesley says, 'At about a quarter before nine, while he was describing the change which God works in the heart through faith in Christ, I felt my heart strangely warmed. I felt I did trust in Christ, Christ alone, for salvation; and assurance was given me that He had taken away my sins, even mine, and saved me from the law of sin and death.'

In the summer of 1738, Wesley spent three months in

Germany visiting the Moravians in their community at Herrnhut, and their leader, Count Nicolaus Zinzendorf. The Moravians played an important part in John Wesley's life at this period, and they also were one of the main factors in the early days of the Evangelical Revival. The secret of the Moravians' influence can be traced back to 1727. Count Zinzendorf had opened his estates to Protestant refugees of various persuasions, but bitter disputing and doctrinal wrangling and an absence of brotherly love threatened to tear the community asunder. Zinzendorf gave himself wholly to a ministry of reconciliation and prayed most earnestly for peace among these warring brotherly factions. He was big enough to recognise the honest intent and deep convictions behind the quarrels. He was able to say of one of the most impetuous of them, 'Although our dear Christian David was calling me the Beast and Mr. Rothe the False Prophet, we could see his honest heart nevertheless, and knew we could lead him right. It is not a bad maxim, when honest men are going wrong, to put them into office, and they will learn from experience what they will never learn from speculation.' Blessed are the peacemakers, and blessed indeed was Zinzendorf. On the 12th May, 1727, they all, with great joy, gave themselves afresh to God and promised to bury their differences and live in peace. A. Bost in *History of the Moravians* says, 'From that time there was a wonderful effusion of the Spirit on this happy church, until August 13th when the measure of divine grace seemed absolutely overflowing.'

The three months from their reconciliation had been filled with prayer and this climax at a communion service on the 13th August 'has rightly been described as a modern Pentecost' says Skevington Wood. The whole gathering was reduced to tears as the Spirit of God moved wonderfully and mightily upon them. The fire of God fell and they left the gathering charged with spiritual power, hardly knowing whether they were in heaven or on earth.

Five days later on the 18th August a remarkable revival occurred among the children at Herrnhut; the Spirit of God so moved upon them that they passed the whole night in prayer. A week later on the 25th August the brethren at Herrnhut began the ministry of continual prayer which continued for over a hundred years. Four years later in 1731 the Moravian missionary outreach began which took Moravians to nearly all parts of the world.

Understandably, John Wesley was greatly helped and deeply impressed by this three months at Herrnhut and he returned strengthened in his conviction as to the essence of the gospel of God's grace and the secret of divine power. After that New Year's Day of Pentecostal blessing in 1739, John Wesley and George Whitefield were both fired with a new heaven-inspired aggression. J. C. Ryle observes, 'They did not wait for sinners to come to them, they pursued them everywhere . . . like men storming a breach . . . no sinner was safe anywhere!' The role was reversed: all heaven was let loose upon Britain in 1739.

Arnold Dallimore writes of Whitefield, 'He possessed a conviction that multitudes of people would be brought into the hearing of the Gospel and, moved by the prospect, began to envisage a new means of reaching them.' As more and more indignant clergy slammed church doors in their faces, the two 'Ws' – Whitefield and John Wesley – turned to preaching in the open-air. 'Field preaching' was the in-phrase of those times, and one can readily see why. England's population was then only around five and a half million and there were no macadamed roads. To preach in the open air mostly meant a field – and they were plentiful.

Whitefield determined to preach at Moorfields, even though he was told he would never come out alive! Moorfields was then a 'baser kind of Hampstead Heath, a great place for Londoners' promenades, pleasure and sports, with space for fairs and circuses, boxing booths, stands and stalls for quacks and rogues of every kind.' But Whitefield never shirked a challenge. The careful evangelical historian, E. M. Poole-Connor, says of Whitefield's first preaching at Moorfield on Sunday, 29th April, 'Even in a life full of revival experiences, this was a special day of God's right hand, a Gospel triumph indeed. He was listened to with great attention by some twenty thousand persons. There was an awed silence while he preached for an hour and a half. Hundreds sought him after his preaching, seeking for salvation.' That was only the beginning, for similar scenes were re-enacted in Hackney Fields, Marylebone Fields, May Fair, Smithfield, Blackheath and Kennington Common. Wherever idle crowds gathered, Whitefield was there. To adapt a famous phrase, 'Never in the field of divine conflict for the souls of men, was so much achieved, by so few, against so many odds, in such a short time, since the days of the Apostles.'

Nor was the impact that of the spoken word only. 'God is pleased to give a great blessing to my printed sermons,' said Whitefield, 'they are in the hands of thousands in these parts, and are a means of enlightening and building up many in the most holy faith . . .' (*The Great Awakening* by Joseph Tracy).

Wesley was a very different character to Whitefield and it was a tremendous step for him to follow Whitefield and preach in the open-air. Wesley was by nature extremely fastidious; he could not bear a speck of dirt on his clerical attire; the dapper little Oxford don hated noise and disturbance. The churchman in Wesley still rebelled at preaching except in churches (although more and more churches were closing their doors to him) and it was with a great deal of reluctance that he accepted Whitefield's invitation to take over from him at Kingswood, Bristol, where Whitefield had been so successful in preaching to the miners. Whitefield had started preaching in open fields to the Kingswood coal-miners in February. Commencing with some two hundred, by March the numbers had risen to twenty thousand and dramatic conversions were taking place. Wesley recorded in his journal, 'It was on the 2nd April, 1739, from a small rise that at four in the afternoon I submitted to be more vile and proclaimed in the highways the glad tidings of salvation.' In 1738 Wesley found his message; in 1739 he found the method – the open-air – and he sustained it for the next half-century. Like Whitefield, he met with immediate success in preaching to the masses and, as with the Master, the common people heard him gladly. Indeed he soon established such a rapport with these rough miners that after his preaching the grimy men gathered around him and clapped him on the back in warm appreciation – like a modern day crowd with a successful soccer star after a great match!

In June 1739, Wesley returned to London having acquired an appetite for open-air preaching. Only some five feet five inches tall and never more than nine stone in weight, with long hair curling down to his shoulders, he commanded attention and almost invariably got it. Quite frequently as he preached, men and women were made to cry out in agony as they came under conviction by the Spirit of God. Sometimes their cries drowned him, and many actually fell prostrate under God's power. Fortunately for posterity, Wesley was one of the greatest diarists of all time and his journal records, 'They dropped on every side as thunderstruck.' But as he applied the healing oil of the gospel of God's grace and love these wounded souls began to rejoice. This amazed Wesley at first; it was beyond even his expectations. This was revival. This was proof that the Spirit of God had anointed him to preach the gospel to the poor. As the years passed the prostrations and more extravagant phenomena decreased. There actually seemed to be more of them under Wesley's preaching than Whitefield's. Perhaps

Arnold Dallimore is right when he says that this was because 'with Whitefield's preaching emotion was freely expressed, while in that of John Wesley it was largely pent up.' But that is almost certainly over-simplifying things. Every revival seems to produce a crop of such unusual occurrences. Deep conviction is the hallmark of the Spirit's work.

On the 15th August in that momentous year of 1739, George Whitefield sailed for America once more. He arrived in Philadelphia daring to believe that God would use his preaching to unite the thirteen scattered colonies to create one nation under God. His faith was not disappointed. Whitefield's arrival fanned the flames of the awakening which had started in 1734 and then had partially subsided. Skevington Wood says, 'It is quite impossible to calculate the full impact of Whitefield's advent. Its effect was immediate, startling and far reaching. The wider work in New England from 1740–43 constituted the American revival proper and is rightly entitled the Great Awakening. Jonathan Edwards was a key figure, but the major influence was that of George Whitefield.'

During this extensive tour of the colonies he preached to vast crowds of many thousands at Philadelphia, New York, and on the famous Boston Common. The meeting at a clearing near Nottingham, Delaware, on May 14th, 1740, was a time of special power. An estimated twelve thousand people gathered. Thousands cried out almost drowning his voice as the Spirit of God gripped them with conviction. George felt and knew that this was the Spirit of God at work in fire and love. Men and women dropped as dead, then revived, then fainted again, as George preached on.

His tour of New England was 'the most remarkable and widespread quickening the American colonies had known' (Skevington Wood). In the space of one chapter it is impossible to do justice to this great servant of God;

his life was one of almost continuous blessing, with real revival manifest on an exceptional number of occasions.

However, in any account of revivals of the 18th century, one simply cannot leave out the great Cambuslang revival. Soon after returning to England from America in 1741, Whitefield had visited Glasgow and he had strongly influenced the minister of the small village of Cambuslang (about four miles away from Glasgow). In his racy biography of Whitefield, John Pollock says, 'His name was William McCulloch. In the following autumn he emphasised in his parish sermons the need of the new birth, until in February 1742 he convened a special three days for prayer.' The spirit of God began to work and three hundred people were converted in the space of the next few months.

In nearby Kilsyth, his friend James Robe had been preaching the new birth even before Whitefield's visit. In May 1742 he set up little prayer groups. Within a month he was experiencing revival too. It spread through other villages. People were gripped in positive agonies of conviction; some were prostrated. And so these two ministers wrote, urgently begging Whitefield to join them at Cambuslang.

Amazing scenes followed. When Whitefield arrived on a Sunday at noon he saw an entire hillside, overlooking the Clyde, covered with worshippers assembled for the quarterly communion. Tents had been erected. Whitefield preached three times that day: at two in the afternoon, at six in the evening and again at nine at night. Afterwards he wrote, 'Such a commotion surely never was heard of. It far outdid all that I ever saw in America. For about an hour and a half there was such weeping, so many falling into deep distress.' Some prayed all night, but the end was not yet. A week later Whitefield returned for another 'specially arranged communion.' On the Saturday he found a congregation of twenty thousand assembled. Pollock writes, 'they seemed charged with divine electricity, a Pentecostal power which astonished even Whitefield.' On the Sunday, still greater crowds gathered, of possibly up to 50,000, for the largest sacrament ever seen in Scotland. Under the open canopy of heaven, and under the panoply of His power, Whitefield ministered and God worked mightily. As Pollock says, 'The Cambuslang work has an undying fame in Scotland's story.'

Both Whitefield and Wesley suffered more than their share of persecution and violent opposition from the mobs in the open-air. Rotten eggs, stones and dead cats were thrown at them. On several occasions their lives were endangered. When Whitefield was forty-two years old he almost became a martyr, when preaching in Dublin. He wrote, 'Volleys of stones came from all quarters and every step I took a fresh stone struck and made me reel backwards and forwards, till I was almost breathless, and all over a gore of blood. I received many blows and wounds; one was particularly large near my temples.'

Wesley also came very near to death in Walsall, in October 1743, at the hands of an enraged mob who cried out, 'Drown him! Hang him!' and even, 'Crucify him!' Some shouted, 'Strip him, tear off his clothes!', to which he mildly responded, 'That you need not do: I will give you my clothes if you want them.' One violent blow made his nose and mouth gush with blood, but he testified afterwards that he felt no pain, and could well understand that the martyrs on occasion had felt no pain in the flames. He was eventually rescued by the very man who had led the mob. 'Sir, I will spend my life for you,' he said. 'Follow me and not one soul here shall touch a hair of your head.' He lifted Wesley on his shoulders and waded through the river to safety.

These two great men allowed nothing and no-one to deter them from their supreme task of 'preaching Christ and bringing men and women to a saving knowledge of His love'. It was a sad day for both of them when they parted asunder over their doctrinal differences, but they retained an abiding respect and love for each other to the end. For Whitefield this came much sooner than Wesley; Whitefield literally burned himself out in his unsparing service for God. He preached his last sermon at the age of fifty-five at Exeter in the United States and he spoke for nearly two hours. After preaching he rode on his horse to Newbury Port where he said, 'Lord Jesus, I am weary in Thy work, but not of Thy work.' He died at Newbury Port, near Boston, September 30th, 1770 and there he was buried.

When Wesley's notable career came to a close in 1791 he had travelled 250,000 miles, preached 40,000 sermons, left about 140,000 Methodist members, as well as some 1500 travelling preachers and had become the instrument of the awakening of innumerable souls.

Arnold Dallimore gives it as his considered opinion that, 'As an evangelical revival it must be considered the greatest since the Apostles.'

The final test of revival as to its genuineness is not the unusual phenomena which occur but the lasting conversions and the effect on society. The awakening under Wesley and Whitefield fully satisfies these requirements. Their ministry undoubtedly changed the face of the United Kingdom and America. Wesley said he did not judge his work by the unusal phenomena that occurred during the high days of revival, but by changed lives. He claimed, 'I will show you him that was a lion – now a lamb; a drunkard – now sober; a whoremonger – now pure. These are my living arguments for what I assert.'

American President Calvin Coolidge once said, 'America was born in a Revival of Religion – and back of it were John Wesley and George Whitefield.'

5

The Ranters' Revival 1800–30

Hugh Bourne and William Clowes

It is almost unbelievable that within sixteen years of the death of John Wesley, the Methodist Conference would expel some of its most zealous sons for holding 'camp meetings' without their permission, and for resisting Conference's attempts to control open-air preaching. But happen it did and the result was the rise of Primitive Methodism. The chief instruments in this glorious revival were Hugh Bourne and William Clowes, two totally opposite characters, but both in the true spiritual lineage of John Wesley.

Hugh Bourne was born at the isolated Fordhay's Farm, Stoke-on-Trent, on April 3rd, 1772. His father was a farmer, timber merchant and wheelwright. Hugh was a deeply thoughtful person but extremely shy; so shy indeed that he would often speak with his hand before his face. He found peace with God only after a long and weary search of twenty years. It was through a printed sermon of Wesley's that he eventually realised true religion was a matter of the heart. He was also influenced by the Quakers, whose strong faith, patience in suffering and zeal for open-air preaching he greatly admired. In 1799 through the writings of another great Methodist saint, John Fletcher's *Letters on the Spiritual Manifesta-*

tion of the Son of God, he at last entered into an experience of peace and assurance that marked his conversion. His own account states, 'I believed in my heart, grace descended and Jesus Christ manifested Himself to me. My sins were taken away in that instant and I was filled with all the joy and peace in believing. I never knew or thought anyone could, in this world, have such a foretaste of Heaven. In an instant I felt I loved God with all my heart, mind, soul and strength, and I felt a love to all mankind, and a desire that all – whether friends or enemies – might be saved. I heard an inward voice saying, "Thy iniquity is forgiven and thy sin covered." Life, light, liberty flowed in upon my soul and such rapturous joy that I could not tell whether in the body or not.'

He joined the Methodist Society at Ridgway, near Bemersley, and was soon exercising an effective ministry among the rough and illiterate miners at Harriseahead, near Mow Cop. One of his first converts was his cousin, Daniel Shubotham, a boxer, poacher and heavy drinker. He was a leading man in crime – a typical example of the degraded community where he lived. Daniel immediately witnessed boldly to his card-playing companions. Hugh Bourne was greatly encouraged and soon another converted miner, Matthias Bayley, joined them in their evangelistic efforts. A local revival ensued in which quite a number of notorious characters in Harriseahead and its surrounds trusted in Christ and were transformed.

Up to this time the only Methodist in Harriseahead was Jane Hall, a very devout woman. A weekly prayer meeting was started in her cottage and at the first meeting, Hugh Bourne, who up until then had been too shy to pray in public, found the courage to do so and 'broke through splendidly'. Despite his shyness, with his experience and knowledge of books, Hugh Bourne was soon the acknowledged leader of the group.

New converts were encouraged to share their new

found faith with their former companions and soon the revival was in progress around Mow Cop. The cottage prayer meetings were the chief means by which the work increased, and they were lively and earnest affairs. Class meetings were established for the guidance and encouragement of the new converts; Daniel Shubotham was appointed leader of the Harriseahead class and Hugh Bourne took the over-sight at Kidsgrove.

Hugh (along with all the converts) was a 'conversation preacher'; they gossipped the gospel at every opportunity to all and sundry, but it was not until July 1801 that he first ventured to preach 'in the pulpit way'. The invitation was for him to preach at the house of Joseph Pointon, on the Cheshire side of Mow. Hugh wanted the service to be in the open air, but Mr. Pointon – in common with the conventional Methodists – was strongly opposed to this procedure. However, such a large crowd assembled that it was impossible for them all to get in the house. Mr. Pointon bowed to the inevitable and so it was that, most appropriately, Hugh Bourne's first sermon was preached in the open-air. It also happened that the field where the service was held was the one where the first English camp meeting was to be held six years later.

It was an epoch-making day, although the strain on the shy Hugh Bourne was tremendous and there was a moment when he was lost for words, but he soon overcame this trying moment and preached acceptably on 'The Faith of Noah' from Hebrews 11:7. Nevertheless, he preached the whole time with his left hand in front of his face with his fingers stretched out and he peered through them as from a barred window – an attitude which he maintained more or less throughout the whole of his ministry.

The increase in the work called for a building and, after many difficulties, a new chapel was erected at Harriseahead. The revival was still nominally a Methodist one, but with little control on the part of the circuit authorities.

A second breath of revival came about through the preaching of sanctification by some revivalists at Congleton. Hugh Bourne sought and obtained the blessing, entering into a deeper spiritual experience. The message of entire sanctification now became prominent in his preaching and as he shared with his fellow workers he says, 'The Holy Spirit descended in such a degree that we began again and again, and for some time could scarce stand or speak, so great was the power of God upon us.' This fresh move of the Spirit of God resulted in the greater part of the Burslem Methodist Circuit being quickened into new life and before long William Clowes, along with others, was converted.

William Clowes was born at Burslem on the 12th March, 1780. His family was quite well-connected but had come down in the world somewhat through the bad habits of his father. His mother's maiden name was Ann Wedgwood, and she was related to Josiah Wedgwood, manufacturer of the famous Wedgwood ware. William was apprenticed as a young boy to his uncle, Josiah Wedgwood, and soon proved himself an expert in the potter's art. He had a vivacious and attractive personality, but unfortunately he was soon following in his father's bad footsteps. A natural leader, he gathered pleasure-loving companions around him. He loved dancing and as a prize dancer he challenged all England. Fighting, gambling, drinking, swearing and profane mockery marked his youth. But when he was twenty-five years of age the Spirit of God began a work in his life. After a short time of conviction as to his wasted youth, he was converted in a Methodist prayer meeting. 'What is this?' he asked himself, 'This is what Methodists mean by being converted: yes, this is it – God is converting my soul. In an agony of prayer I believed God would save me – then I believed He was saving me – then I believed He had saved me, and it was so.'

William Clowes' conversion was dramatic in its suddenness. He paid up his debts, opened his house for prayer meetings, started giving out religious tracts, went from house to house witnessing, and soon became a class leader and a local preacher. The revival continued to spread around Tunstall and Mow Cop, and Bourne and Clowes became friends. They were a perfect foil for each other: Clowes was an extremely gifted and out-going personality with music in his soul and voice, imaginative and fluent; whereas Bourne was more thoughtful and mentally disciplined with outstanding gifts of organisation.

The prayer meetings were times of real power with the newly converted miners eager to start praying and reluctant to stop. Time was always precious as these miners had to be at work very early in the morning, consequently there was not always opportunity for all of them to pray. On one occasion when there was some good-natured grumbling by those who had not had chance to pray, Daniel Shubotham remarked 'You shall have a whole day's praying on Mow some Sunday and then you'll be satisfied.' He little realised the prophetic significance of that remark.

Mow Cop is the highest point of the south-westernmost ridge of the Pennine range; the name was formerly Mole or Mael, signifying 'bald', while Cop simply means 'peak'. It is 1,100 feet high and forms a landmark for miles around. It has been aptly called the Mount Carmel of Primitive Methodism. Just when the revival fires were dying down a little there was a providential visit from a Lorenzo Dow. Dow, a somewhat eccentric though vivid and powerful personality, was an unattached Methodist and newly returned from America where he had been greatly thrilled by their great camp meetings. When he visited Harriseahead in April 1807 he enthused about these meetings, claiming that occasionally 'something of a Pentecostal Power attended them and that, for a considerable time in America, as much good had been done and as many souls brought to God at camp meetings as at all the other meetings put together.'

The description captured the imagination of Hugh Bourne and he purposed to hold a camp meeting at Norton during the August wakes, the specific idea being to meet the Devil on his own ground. But when he put the proposal to his local fellowship they were too eager to wait until August. Daniel Shubotham examined the circuit preaching plan and when he noted that Thomas Cotton was planned on 31st May, he instantly exclaimed, 'That's the camp meeting!' The decision aroused widespread interest and people travelled from miles around for the historic, first organised English camp meeting. They came from Macclesfield, Warrington, Stockport and further afield, many travelling all night to be on the spot by early morning. They gathered in a field on the Cheshire side of Mow and an improvised flag was hoisted to mark the 'preaching stand'. Praying, singing, preaching, exhortation and testimony blended in this unusual meeting. Informal, unconventional, orderly and yet disorderly; nothing like it had been seen in England before.

This is how William Clowes described that momentous day. 'The first day's praying on Mow Hill presented at this period a most magnificent and sublime spectacle. Four preachers simultaneously crying to sinners to flee from the wrath to come; thousands listening, affected by "thoughts that breathe and words that burn"; many in deep distress and others pleading with Heaven on their behalf; some praising God aloud for the great things which were brought to pass, whilst others were rejoicing in the testimony which they had received, that their sins had all been forgiven. The camp meeting continued full of glory and converting power.'

The success of Mow Cop led to other camp meetings but Methodist officialdom did not appreciate the new wine. The Wesleyan Conference ruled such meetings as perhaps 'allowable in America but highly improper in England,' and 'disclaimed all connection with them.' This shattering decision was pressed home by the Superintendent of the circuit and even Daniel Shubotham and William Clowes bowed to the official decision for a time. But Hugh Bourne 'after much mental conflict, came to the conclusion that he must continue them as calculated to do much good!' For this he was expelled from the Wesleyan body in 1808. When Clowes decided to take his stand with Bourne he also suffered the same fate in 1810. They continued their evangelistic labours and met with greater success than ever; many converts were made and new societies were formed.

There was still no idea of a new denomination and the converts were placed under the care of the Wesleyans. The issue came to a head, however, when the Wesleyan officials refused to accept ten new converts at Standley: converts 'raised out of the world by Bourne and his helpers.' They were therefore forced to go it alone and they became known at first in 1810 as the Camp Meeting Methodists.

Mention must be made of the influence of James Crawfoot, the leader of the 'Magic Methodists' as they were termed. He had been a Methodist local preacher, but on account of his association with the Quaker Methodists he had been expelled in 1807. He had, however, gathered around him a band of ardent disciples who rallied to monthly meetings held in his own house in the forest. Crawfoot was known to be versed in the deep things of God. Bourne and Clowes were greatly helped by this Christian mystic. George Herod said, 'Crawfoot's home was the college in which Clowes received instruction. We candidly acknowledge that Clowes was under a great obligation to the old man of the forest, and that much which he taught in the infancy of Primitive Methodism can be traced to this source. Crawford taught Clowes the law of faith, the method of opening Heaven in prayer, and bringing down an influence that caused believers to thirst for more purity of heart and sinners to grieve for their sins.' In Crawfoot's monthly meetings his followers on occasions saw visions as they waited upon God in prayer; they were also caught up in raptures of ecstasy and even fell into trances – they were not afraid of the movings of the Holy Spirit and the power of God was a reality to them.

Hugh Bourne wrote in his journal for 3rd November, 1808 about one of the meetings in Crawfoot's cottage, 'I sat with Crawfoot and others, they were talking and I breathed my soul to God for the Holy Ghost to come upon that church. I turned my head and James Crawfoot was looking at me. His face shone, I could not bear it but was near fainting away. My soul breathed, Lord Jesus, receive my spirit, but I did not go down; nevertheless the Lord made great discoveries to me and I felt resolute to feel after this thing. O Lord, grant it to me for Thy name's sake.'

In May 1811, the new denomination was born, though the name 'Primitive Methodist' was not adopted until February 1812. The name came about from the time James Crawfoot was brought up before the Wesleyan authorities in 1807 and expelled for preaching for the Quaker Methodists. He quoted from one of Wesley's last addresses dated 1790, 'Fellow labourers, wherever there is an open door enter in and preach the Gospel; if it be to two or three, under a hedge or a tree, preach the Gospel; "go out quickly into the street and lanes of the city and bring in hither the poor and the maimed and the halt and the blind; and the servant said, Lord it is done as thou hast commanded, and yet there is room".' Crawfoot then lifted up his hands and with tears flowing down his cheeks, repeated, 'And yet there is room, and yet there is room.' The quotation given, Crawfoot said, 'Mr. Chairman, if you have deviated from the old usages, I have not; I still remain a Primitive Methodist.' This was the characteristic of the men at the heart of the beginning of the Primitive Methodist revival. Crawfoot was financially supported by Hugh Bourne and his brother and became the first travelling evangelist, which he continued to be until 1813.

Great camp meetings were held in various parts of the country. They attracted large crowds and were a great means of the work growing and spreading. The English camp meetings were never camp meetings in the same sense as the American ones. The English ones were much more haphazard, less organised, more flexible. Nevertheless some of them were times of real revival power when the Spirit of God was poured out upon the many thousands who gathered. Some of the famous ones were at Wrekin, Shropshire in 1808; Nottingham Forest in 1816; Scarth Nick in 1820; Mexborough Common in 1821; Oakengates and Oldham in 1822; and Winchester Downs in 1834. H. B. Kendall observes, 'At some of these from ten to twenty thousand persons are said to have been present. Again and again there were scenes of Divine demonstration and the power of the Holy Ghost.'

Clowes made rapid progress in the things of God and soon became an outstanding evangelist of great power. What he lacked in statesmanship and organising ability was supplied by Hugh Bourne who excelled in these qualities, and so the work prospered. Clowes swept across the country like a flame of fire; the new movement swept eastwards along the Vale of Trent until it reached Hull, and there, under Clowes, a revival was experienced which resulted in four hundred members in church fellowship within four months. He moved northward and then westwards until he could preach his way from Hull to Carlisle; there were twenty-one centres with nearly twelve thousand members.

Remarkable spiritual gifts were manifested by many of these Primitive Methodist pioneers. Bourne and Clowes were the undoubted leaders but they were supported by a whole galaxy of unusual characters who displayed amazing individuality and Spirit-inspired originality which proved effective in communicating the gospel to the unchurched multitudes. Many of these anointed preachers were credited with possessing what was then termed second sight (the ability to foresee the future, and see actions taking place elsewhere and so on) but which today most Pentecostals and Charismatics would undoubtedly term 'spiritual gifts' as listed by Paul in I Corinthians 12, especially 'the word of wisdom', or 'the word of knowledge', or 'discerning of spirits'. Such a one was Billy Braithwaite, whom Joseph Ritson describes as 'the Apostle of North Lincoln – quaint, eccentric, with a certain gift of second sight which he possessed in common with not a few of the pioneers, and who prayed, "Lord, give me souls or I shall die". A farmer who overheard left his ploughing to discover who was quarrelling behind the hedge, but found only one man with the tears running down his cheeks. It filled him with wonder and it still rings down the years as a challenge to us all.'

Two other worthies were Thomas Russell and John Ride, who once met on Ashdown Common in Berkshire in the middle of winter. Finding a secluded spot in the wood, oblivious of the snow, they threw themselves upon their knees and in an agony they poured out their souls to God. 'Lord, give us Berkshire!' they pleaded again and again. They prayed for some five hours until at last Thomas Russell (termed by Ritson 'the Apostle of Berkshire') sprang to his feet and pointed to the distant horizon and triumphantly cried, 'Yonder country is ours and we will take it.' Until then the violent and devilish opposition had prevented progress, but from that day the victory was theirs and a great revival followed. In the end there were more Primitive Methodist congregations in Berkshire than any other Nonconformist Church.

There were many other heroes of faith such as Thomas Batty, the Apostle of Weardale, whose marvellous revival won the fair Dales of the North for Christ and Primitive Methodism; and Joseph Spoor, from Whickham, near Newcastle-on-Tyne, whose spiritual power, mingled with humour and unorthodox originality, made him famous all over the North-East.

The name of Johnny Oxtoby, affectionately known as Praying Johnny, cannot however be excluded. Johnny had the kind of faith that moves mountains and every day he spent hours on his knees. The story of his pleading for Filey is now legendary. Filey in Yorkshire had resisted the brave efforts of many preachers and each one had been driven out until the Conference decided to abandon it. Johnny Oxtoby pleaded that they should give it one more try, and expressed his firm conviction that God would yet manifest Himself there. He himself undertook the mission and when he arrived at Muston Hill, within sight of Filey, he fell on his knees in agony of soul. Under a hedge he wrestled in prayer and wept and interceded for the success of his mission. A passing miller heard his voice and stopped in astonishment to listen. The miller heard Johnny Oxtoby say, 'Thou munna make a fool o' me, God. I told them at Bridlington that Thou wast going to revive Thy work, and Thou must do, or I shall never be able to show my face among them again, and then what will the people say about praying and believing?' He continued to plead for several hours. The struggle was long and heavy but he would not give in. At last he rose exclaiming, 'It is done, Lord, Filey is taken! Filey is taken!' And it was. Fresh from the presence of God he entered Filey and commenced singing in the streets. 'Turn to the Lord and seek salvation,' was his theme and soon a crowd of rough fishermen flocked to listen. Unusual power attended his preaching and these strong fishermen trembled, hardened sinners wept and while he prayed, over a dozen of them fell on their knees and cried aloud for mercy and found it.

The nickname 'Ranters' was given them at Belper,

Derbyshire, on account of their loud voices and lively singing. Like the first Methodists they were attacked by mobs with stones and rotten eggs and filth. They were ridiculed, persecuted, and unjustly imprisoned, but they refused to be silenced. The Primitive Methodist Chapels became notorious as centres of 'converting power' and the preachers were called 'the now preachers' from their insistence on pressing for instant response to their message. By the time Bourne and Clowes retired in 1842 the Prims. had 1,278 chapels and 85,565 members. By the end of the nineteenth century the membership had reached 212,000.

They loved to preach, pray, shout and sing; quaint hymns with lilting tunes were a unique feature of their meetings. But the depth and reality of the revival is vouched for by their effect on society. In common with John Wesley and the first Methodists who, in the opinion of many, saved Britain from revolution in the 18th century, there are reliable historians who claim that the Prims, likewise saved Britain from revolution in the 19th century, by converting the ringleaders of violence and anarchy in thousands of parishes all over the country. They rendered great service to Trade Unionism, temperance, education and social services. At the centenary of the first camp meeting, one hundred thousand people assembled in May 1907 for a great camp meeting. The final proof of revival is the power of the Holy Spirit bringing souls to new birth, resulting in changed lives which in turn affect and improve society.

6

The 1858 Awakening in America

James Burns in *Revival, Their Laws and Leaders* says that preceding revivals, there often seems to be 'a widespread spirit of dissatisfaction among those God is preparing for what He is about to do. The heart of man begins to cry out for God, for spiritual certainties, for fresh visions. From a faint desire this multiplies as it widens, until it becomes a vast human need; until in its urgency it seems to beat with violence at the very gates of Heaven.'

Such was the situation before the great 1858 Awakening in America. For more than ten years things had been spiritually at a low ebb. William Miller, the Adventist founder, had brought ridicule on the churches by fixing 1843 as the date for Christ's return. In the business world the financial boom collapsed and recession followed.

Spurgeon in one of his Revival Year Sermons of 1859 asked, 'Have you ever heard of the great 1858 American Revival? An obscure man laid it up in his heart to pray that God would bless his country.' That man was Jeremiah Lanphier, a newly appointed city missioner in a downtown New York church which was suffering the effects of population migration. Born in Coxsackie, upper New York in 1809, Lanphier had been converted in 1842 in Broadway Tabernacle (which had been built

by the great revivalist, Charles Finney, ten years earlier).
He was a man of prayer, an effective speaker and a man
with plenty of energy. Burdened by the need around
him, he decided to invite others to join him in a noonday
prayer meeting every Wednesday in Fulton Street. He
had some hand-bills printed inviting 'merchants,
mechanics, clerks, strangers and businessmen generally'
to join him in 'calling upon God'. It was timed to last one
hour, with the usual proviso for such mid-day meetings
that people were free to come when they could and go
when they must.

Lanphier opened the doors for the first meeting on
23rd September, 1857 at noon and waited for the people
to come in. 'Five minutes went by; twenty minutes;
twenty-five; thirty – and then at 12.30 p.m. he heard a
step on the stairs and the first person joined him. A few
moments later there was another, and another, until they
numbered six and the prayer meeting began. On the following Wednesday the six had increased to twenty; on
the third week there were forty intercessors,' says Edwin
Orr in his great book *The Second Evangelical Awakening*.

The decision was then taken to hold the prayer meeting daily, and the same week news came of an extraordinary revival in Hamilton, Ontario, Canada. Under the
ministry of evangelists Walter and Phoebe Palmer, some
three or four hundred people of all classes were converted. Attendances reached six thousand and virtually
the whole of the community was affected from the mayor
and people of high estate down to servants and children.
The revival was spontaneous and especially stirred the
laity into activity and Christian service. The Hamilton
revival was widely reported in Christian newspapers and
aroused the desires of many Christians in America.

The week following, there was a great financial crash
and an ensuing panic as banks failed, following a year of
recession. The atmosphere was ripe for God to move.
Who better than Spurgeon to describe and assess the

situation? In the sermon previously mentioned he said, 'The prayer meeting grew to a hundred, then others began to start prayer-meetings; at last there was scarcely a street in New York that was without a prayer meeting. Merchants found time in the middle of the day to pray. The prayer meetings became daily ones, lasting for about an hour. Petitions and requests were sent up – these were simply asked and offered before God, and the answers came – many stood up and testified that the prayer offered last week had already been fulfilled.'

By the beginning of 1858, the Fulton Street prayer meeting was so crowded that they were trying to accommodate the numbers by holding three simultaneous prayer meetings in rooms on different floors in the same building. Prayer became the order of the day. In March, a noon prayer meeting was commenced in a large theatre. Half an hour before the announced time it was packed out – the great majority being men – businessmen! Three days later the outstanding preacher Henry Ward Beecher led three thousand in that theatre prayer meeting. The newspapers began to sit up and take notice and to report on the happenings. It was front page news that over six thousand were attending daily prayer meetings in New York.

The river of revival blessing was at the flood and soon it burst it banks and flowed across the nation, until literally every part of the American nation was affected. Other great cities like Boston, Chicago, Washington, Buffalo, Newark, soon had their noon-day prayer meetings too. It became a common sight to see businesses closed with a notice: 'Will re-open at the close of the prayer meeting.'

Sometimes, as in Philadelphia, things started slowly. A young man aged 21, after being in the great New York prayer meetings, returned to his home city of Philadelphia and gained permission to start a prayer meeting in a room at a Methodist Church, on 23rd November, 1857.

For three months, only about a dozen people came, but in February the meeting place was changed and attendances increased to sixty. In March the wave of revival poured over the city and soon some 6,000 were gathering daily for prayer. In the capital, Washington, five daily prayer meetings were launched commencing respectively at 6.30 a.m., 10 a.m., noon, 5 p.m. and 7 p.m.; by April, thousands were attending.

One sure test of revival is the number and quality of converts which result. Those 'born in the fire' seem to have a special stamp upon them that remains. Though revival always begins with the quickening of believers, it must culminate with the conversion of unbelievers.

The Great Awakening of 1858 is unusual even among revivals in several ways. It was wonderfully and happily free from fanaticism. Equally remarkably it was also free from personality adulation. As Edwin Orr comments, 'The revival produced no great leaders immediately.' Even so the work spread apace like a prairie fire.

In Kalamazoo, Michigan, all the main Protestant bodies united for prayer. At the first gathering the following request was read, 'A praying wife requests the prayers of this meeting for her unconverted husband.' A burly man stood up and blurted, 'I am that man. I have a praying wife and this request must be for me. I want you to pray for me.' No sooner had he sat down than another man arose with sobs and tears to claim, 'I am sure I am that man, and I want you to pray for me.' He was not the last either for soon another three 'convicted husbands' were on their feet asking for prayer. The power of God fell upon that gathering and soon there were over 400 conversions in the town. One of the most colourful converts was a boxer, Orville Gardner, better known as 'Awful' Gardner. News of his conversion and his testimony given in public influenced many, especially the sporting types.

By May it was reliably estimated that there were

50,000 conversions in New York; the population of which was then around 800,000. In New England it seemed that the impact was even greater. One reporter noted, 'The chief concern here is religion. Meetings are usually crowded and solemn, with the whole assembly sometimes in tears under the melting power of the Holy Spirit.' In a few months thousands of converts were added to the churches. The same newspaper reported, 'There are several New England towns in which not a single adult person can be found unconverted.'

True revival must always have a definite impact on society as a whole and that is just what happened in 1858. In Louisville, Kentucky, there was such an improvement in the city's morals that the press thought the millennium had arrived. One described it: 'The Spirit of God seems to be brooding over our city and to have produced an unusual degree of tenderness and solemnity in all classes.' In the West, converts were so in earnest that in winter the ice was broken on the Mohawk River for believers to be baptised by immersion.

Every stratum of society was touched. An atmosphere of great stillness and solemnity often prevailed. In Newark, a leading minister testified that the most mature minds in the community were being won to Christ and the most mature personalities in his own congregation were the forty-five who had just united with it by profession of faith in Christ. In New England especially the colleges were blessed. The famous Yale University had such a visitation that it was impossible to estimate the number of conversions, and the president of Amherst College declared that nearly all the students had been converted.

In the revival in Hamilton, Canada, it was the laity who took the lead. It was a move of God that started at the grass-roots with 'ordinary believers', those in the pew rather than the pulpit. This same characteristic also marked the revival in America. Finney wrote of this revival, 'This winter of 1857–58 will be remembered as the time when a great revival prevailed. It swept over the land with such power, that for a time it was estimated that not less than 50,000 conversions occurred weekly.' The lay influence predominated to such an extent that ministers were overshadowed. This awakening was not 'a remote piety in little corners' of churches, but to the fore of everyday business life, college life and home life; it was right there in the 'nitty-gritty' of work-a-day life, not just a Sunday affair.

The revival became known as the 'prayer meeting revival' from its being marked far and wide by fervent prayer. The results of the awakening were abiding. Edwin Orr, after a long and careful researching, endorses the estimate 'that fully one million were converted out of a population of less than thirty million, in the revival in the two-year period 1858–59.' The churches actually increased their membership by this figure. These were not the disappearing assets of mere decisions which so often today vanish overnight, but solid, lasting and real converts.

All the major Protestant denominations benefited. There was a wonderful spirit of co-operation between all Christians; it was thoroughly interdenominational. This was doubtless one factor which resulted in the secular press giving full coverage to the revival, which also assisted in the spreading of the blessing. Those involved said that a divine influence seemed to pervade the land; as the Spirit of God moved upon people their hearts were warmed towards God and their fellow men. A leading Methodist paper (*The Methodist Advocate* – January 1858) reported ten noteworthy features of the revival: 1. Few sermons had to be preached; 2. Lay brethren were eager to witness; 3. Seekers flocked to the altar; 4. Nearly every seeker had been blessed; 5. Experiences enjoyed remained clear; 6. Converts were filled with holy boldness; 7. Religion became a day-time social topic; 8. Family altars were strengthened; 9. Testimony given nightly was abundant; 10. Conversation was marked by a pervading seriousness.

Not only were the churches blessed with one million new converts, but as Edwin Orr points out, they were 'reinvigorated by one million nominal church members being revived!' A million revived church members, plus one million new converts. No wonder that many capable Christian leaders gave it as their judgement that it was the most widespread awakening America had experienced. The results were nation-wide and ultimately world-wide.

7

Ulster 1859

It is always a fascinating exercise to seek to trace the wonderful workings of the Spirit of God in revival. As the Saviour Himself declared, the movings of the Holy Spirit are as mysterious as the wind. Yet, as with the wind, men have discovered definite and discernible patterns, so with the wind of God's Spirit, there is sufficient divine direction to enable seeking souls to set their sails aright.

From the human standpoint it often seems that revival spreads like a forest fire, spreading from place to place, sometimes leaping ahead over an area by sparks carried ahead of the main fire by especially strong gusts of wind. On the other hand, when comparing revival accounts one often discovers that simultaneously in various parts of the world, without any human link, God's Spirit was at work. Such instances can only be described as cases of divine spontaneous combustion.

Ireland has many links with America and it was not surprising that news of the great revival in America in 1858 soon spread to Ulster as Irish-Americans wrote home to their relatives. The stories of the American Awakening created a great longing for a similar visitation of God in Ireland and people started to pray. However, it is interesting and significant to note that the very month Jeremiah Lanphier commenced the Fulton Street Prayer

Meeting in New York, September 1857, four young Irishmen began a weekly prayer meeting in a village school near Kells, not far from Ballymena. This meeting is generally regarded as the origin of the 1859 Revival which swept 100,000 converts into the churches in Ireland.

The names of those four are rightly remembered; they were James McQuilkin, John Wallace, Robert Carlisle and Jeremiah Meneely. McQuilkin was converted in 1856 through the witnessing of a visiting English Christian woman named Mrs. Colville. The young convert read George Muller's autobiography and was deeply impressed by Muller's prayer life and faith. He prayed for a spiritual companion with whom he could pray and God gave him one. The two then prayed together and a further two were added to them. McQuilkin shared with his friends the blessings he had received through reading about Muller and suggested they met for prayer. For a few months they had to walk by faith but they faithfully continued. When James McQuilkin heard of the revival in America he said to himself, 'Why may we not have such a blessed work here?' and he shared his burden and vision with his three praying companions. The fuse was laid. The first conversion in answer to their prayers came in December, 1857. From that time, Reverend W. Gibson says, 'Humble, grateful, loving, joyous converts multiplied'. The prayer meetings became thronged. The fuse was lit.

There were many thousands of Ulster-Americans in the U.S.A. and as the news of the American Awakening continued to reach Ulster, interest was quickened to the point where the General Assembly of the Presbyterian Church in Ireland decided to send two of its most trusted members to investigate. The favourable report of these two godly and trusted men – Professor William Gibson and the Rev. William McClure – promoted the desire for a similar visitation. Throughout the winter months of

1858–59 the praying increased in volume and intensity. Prayer meetings multiplied just as they had done in America. Ministers began to preach on revival; one of such was the Rev. J. H. Moore of Connor, Co. Antrim. For years he had preached the gospel faithfully but with little result. He began to read to his church extracts from the accounts of previous revivals such as under Daniel Rowlands in Wales, Jonathan Edwards in New England, and George Whitefield's glorious days in Scotland, 'until the idea of a great revival took hold of many in the congregation.' Rev. J. H. Moore was amply rewarded, for the revival broke out in Connor. He was able to report, 'There is a network of prayer meetings over the whole district. From first to last the revival was a record of answered prayer. Never was there such a time of secret and public prayer. In all directions prayer meetings have sprung up, and that without number. They are conducted in a manner of deepest solemnity, and with a burning earnestness for the outpouring of the Holy Ghost, and for the conversion of souls. These meetings have been signally honoured of the Lord. The Spirit has descended in power.'

On the 14th, March 1859, at the invitation of the minister of the Ahoghill Presbyterian Church, James McQuilkin and his praying friends organised a great prayer meeting. Such a tremendous crowd pressed into the church that they cleared the building for fear of the galleries collapsing. Outside in the chilling rain, 'a layman' began to preach with such anointing and power that soon hundreds were on their knees in the mud. Edwin Orr in *The Fervent Prayer* says, 'This apparently was the first outbreak of mass conviction of sin to occur anywhere in the British Isles during the mid-nineteenth century awakening about to spread throughout the United Kingdom.'

Just three miles away from Ahogill is the busy market town of Ballymena which then had a population of 6,000. In April 1859, on a crowded market day, a man of about

thirty years of age suddenly fell on his knees and began to
cry aloud. An alarmed crowd ran to him thinking some
terrible accident had occurred. He carried on like this for
some ten minutes and was finally led away by friends to
the house of a relative. As he walked down the street he
repeatedly exclaimed, 'Unclean . . . Lord be merciful to
me a sinner!' Clearly this was no accident but the Spirit
of God doing His mysterious work. One hall mark of true
revival is conviction of sin.

A few weeks later, on May 17th, it seemed the whole
town was in the grip of the Spirit of God's convicting
power. Careless men became earnest about their soul's
salvation and many broke down and sobbed like children. According to one report, 'Ministers who had often
toiled in heartless sorrow suddenly found themselves
beset by enquirers.' Churches were crowded, families
prayed together all classes, all age groups sought the Lord
for salvation and did not seek in vain. Prayer meetings
often carried on all night.

Once started, the revival fires spread rapidly, but
undoubtedly this area in County Antrim: the Parish of
Connor, Ballymena and Kells, was the heart of the
Awakening.

At this period of the revival amazing physical manifestations took place. The principal one was that of people
being physically prostrated. Some regarded this as hys-
teria, but others regarded it as a divine method of conviction. Undoubtedly there were spurious cases, and some
the result of mere human excitement, but one must never
judge revival by our cold, correct formalism. These
prostrations were very different from some current
phenomena of people falling down when prayed for in
healing meetings. Many prostrations in the revival occurred when people were alone. For example, a deaf-mute
was prostrated and converted while working alone in a
bog cutting turf near Balleymoney.

The Rev. J. K. Killen said, 'I am satisfied that these

prostrations have not only been exceedingly useful in the way of arousing and arresting the attention of both the Church and the world, but I am convinced that they have also been greatly blessed to the persons affected.'

A happy feature of the Ulster Revival was the work among the children. Some adults called these physical manifestations – prostrations, swooning, strong shaking, trembling and convulsed weeping – 'sickness'. But a young boy who was deeply convicted of his need of the Saviour said to his father, 'Don't call this taking ill, as if it were sickness, it is just the soul taking Christ.' Whilst another boy said, 'There has been sickness many a time in this country but it never sent people to their prayers.'

Coleraine, also in County Antrim, a few miles north from Ballymena was favoured with special visitations of power and blessing. In one of the large schools a boy came under conviction so much so that the teacher sent him home with an older boy, who had been converted only the previous day. On the way home they turned into an empty house to pray together. The troubled boy was soon rejoicing and said, 'I must go back and tell the teacher.' With a beaming face he told him, 'O Sir, I am so happy; I have the Lord Jesus in my heart.' The whole class was deeply affected as a result and boy after boy rose and silently left the room. When the teacher went to investigate he found them ranged around the playground wall on their knees. Silent prayer soon gave way to loud cries and prayers, which carried to the girls school on the first floor. Immediately the girls fell on their knees and wept. The commotion carried into the street; neighbours and passers-by came flocking in. As soon as they crossed the threshold they all came under the same convicting power. Ministers came to help, men of prayer were summoned and the day was spent in leading young and old to saving faith in Christ. Meals were forgotten and the work continued until 11 p.m. that night.

'On June 7th a great open-air meeting was held in

Coleraine when converts testified. Such great crowds gathered that they were divided into several groups each to be addressed by different ministers. God's presence was an awesome reality. Many came under deep conviction. Many prostrations occurred. It continued throughout the following day, and in the evening the market place was crowded. The gospel was preached and again, 'many sank down to the ground and with bitter cries sought the Lord for mercy. Christian helpers took many of these "stricken ones" as they now began to be called, into the newly completed Town Hall then awaiting "its official opening".' A Bible is still kept there which bears this inscription, 'It is meant to be a memorial of the first opening of the new Town Hall when upon the night of 9th June 1859, nearly one hundred persons, agonised in mind through conviction of sin, and entirely prostrate in body, were borne into that building to obtain shelter during the night, and to receive consolation from the instructions and prayers of Christian ministers and Christian people.'

Converts from the Connor area visited Belfast, then a large town with a population of 120,000. Within a few days the whole community was affected. A few weeks later saw a great gathering of 30,000 in the Botanic Gardens. The work went on unabated throughout the summer months, until all the six northern counties were affected.

Eventually the Southern part of Ireland was also touched. Dublin experienced much blessing and Spurgeon preached in some of the great meetings; there were in those day more Prostestants than now – an estimated 22 per cent in the city itself and no less than 40 per cent in the suburbs. The revival was strongest in Protestant areas, but many Roman Catholics were converted and many abandoned their Catholicism as they embraced the teachings of God's Word. On board the Kingston-Holyhead steamers the revival fervour affected the crew of one boat so that all, apart from three, were converted.

True revival always produces lasting converts and raises the social and moral standard of the community. The 1859 revival brought lasting benefits to the country. A large whisky distillery in Belfast was put up for auction – the trade had so fallen off. In the Connor area two pubs had to close because the publicans had got converted, and a third closed for lack of trade. The Maze Racecourse in October 1859 drew only five hundred people instead of the usual 10,000. Mocking gave way to fear and reverence as the revival progressed. Crime was reduced tremendously. In Coleraine in 1860, the Grand Jury of the Quarter Sessions were informed that crime had been reduced to almost negligible proportions. Throughout Ulster, judges several times found themselves without any cases to try. In County Antrim at one period during the awakening, it was noted that there was not one prisoner in police custody and not one crime reported to the police.

Towards the end of 1860, the effects of the revival were reviewed and summarised as follows: 1. the preaching services were thronged; 2. numbers of communicants were unprecedented; 3. prayer meetings were abundant; 4. family prayers were increased; 5. scripture reading was unmatched; 6. Sunday Schools were prosperous; 7. converts remained generally stedfast; 8. liberality seemed greatly increased; 9. vice was abated; and 10. crime was much reduced. (Quoted by Edwin Orr in *Fervent Prayer* from *Evangelical Christendom* 1860.)

Edwin Orr (himself an Ulsterman) says, 'This revival which originated in a prayer meeting of four young men in the village schoolhouse of Kells made greater impact spiritually on Ireland than anything else known since the days of Saint Patrick.' (*The Fervent Prayer*.)

8

Britain 1859

England, Scotland and Wales were all visited by the Spirit of God in revival blessing around this memorable year of 1859. All were stamped with the same divine authenticity of deep conviction of sin and genuine lasting conversions, but the revival in each of the three countries displayed special features befitting their own national characteristics. The Holy Spirit always honours the individuality of people and nations.

The signal feature in Wales, for example, seemed to be a most glorious rapturous praise which marked the crisis point in each locality. This 'moliannu' or praising, was unique to Wales, a peculiar form of worship involving preacher and people in turn.

This special move of God in Wales also had a definite link with events in America. H. R. Jones had emigrated to America in the mid 1850s and was ordained in the Methodist Episcopal Church. Soon he was personally involved in the revival, and in 1858 he returned to his native Wales, and began to preach with a measure of success. The Rev. David Morgan, a Welsh Calvinistic Methodist, was somewhat sceptical, but on hearing young Jones preach he was greatly moved and within a few days was himself preaching under a new anointing from God. His own village had only a population of a thousand but before the end of the year, 200 converts had been won. The next year, David Morgan began to move in neighbouring villages and towns with great blessing and power. The tide of the Spirit rolled up the Welsh Valleys, higher and higher, until every county in Wales was experiencing the blessing. A week of prayer was held in January 1860, and a second wave swept Wales, with even greater power in many places.

David Morgan's son described the outbreak of revival in a Carmarthenshire town, 'One Sunday morning an elder rose to speak and his first remark was that the God they worshipped was without beginning and without end. "Amen!" exclaimed a young girl in the highest notes of a lovely voice, "Blessed be His name forever!" This cry might be compared to the touch of the electric button that shivers a quarry into a thousand hurtling fragments. Scores leaped from their seats, and, gathering in the vacant space in the centre, they gave vent to their pent-up emotion in outcries that were almost agonising in their ardour and intensity.' Happenings of a similar pattern to this occurred again and again and always with the same result: the already converted section of the congregation engaged in unrestrained ejaculatory praise and the unconverted half fell under the deepest conviction.

For any tempted to dismiss this as Welsh emotionalism, they should note that the results were widespread, beneficial and lasting, encompassing all classes and all kinds of people. There was a move amongst students; a work with soldiers; quarry men of the roughest kind were brought to Christ; seamen were reached; notorious characters of the worst kind were transformed; and at the other end of the scale, children began to pray in a most beautiful and unaffected way. Crime dropped significantly. In 1860 the criminal cases before the Welsh Courts decreased from 1,809 to 1,228. At Menai Bridge, a local policeman was reproved by the Chief Constable for attending prayer meetings. He excused himself by explaining that the roads were quiet and the public houses were empty, and that the chapels were the only places of excitement. The Chief Constable heard that the offending constable had not only attended but had actually prayed in the meeting! Thereupon a red-letter notice was sent to all constables instructing them not to pray in prayer-meetings. The order was disregarded!!

Altogether it is reliably estimated that 100,000 people were added to the churches in Wales, at a time when the total population was about one million.

In Scotland, the time was ripe for a special move of the Spirit of God. There had been several wonderful awakenings during the period 1800 to 1840. For example there was a tremendous revival in 1839 under the preaching of W. C. Burns, to name but one of many Scottish revivalists of this time. But by the 1850s, things for the most part had settled down. Some men of God had however remained faithfully on their watchtowers, praying and longing for a fresh visitation of Almighty God. Men such as the brothers Andrew and Horatius Bonar kept 'the expectant evangelical spirit alive.' Another key figure was Brownlow North, an aristocratic playboy of his day (the grand-nephew of Lord North, the Prime Minister of George III). His dramatic conversion in 1854 at the age of forty-four had rocked society. Within a few years his 'John the Baptist' – like preaching rocked society even more. 'He preached the truth of the living God in a manner scarcely seen since the days of Whitefield,' said one observer.

Unlike Wales, 'the main development of the movement seemed to come from America via Ulster to Scotland,' says Edwin Orr. Prayer in times of revival seems to set off a kind of nuclear chain reaction. For example the Rev. Adam Blyth of Girvan was impressed to find that the great united prayer meeting in New York had been requested to pray for the spiritual needs of Coleraine, Ulster, which became one of the key centres of the Ulster revival. The united prayer meeting in Coleraine was in turn asked to pray for the spiritual welfare of Port Glasgow on the Clyde, which soon afterwards 'was in the throes of a revival.'

Commencing on the West coast of Scotland it had surged through the Border country, flowed over the dour capital of Edinburgh, deluged the growing industrial Glasgow, finally sweeping up into the Highlands, over into the remote Orkneys, and into the Shetlands. As the revival progressed, Brownlow North became one of a trio sometimes called 'the gentlemen evangelists.' Hay Macdowal Grant of Arndilly was another member of it and he, like North, was converted in middle life. He was greatly blessed in personal soul-winning, and spent hours tramping the heather visiting remote cottages and seeking souls for Christ. The third was Reginald Radcliffe, a Christian solicitor mightily used of God.

All sorts of people were reached in the revival: prostitutes, ladies of high rank, schoolboys, millhands, drunkards, gamblers, and even the so-called 'simpletons'. A friend of North in a letter to him wrote, 'One peculiarity of the present movement is the coming of poor simpletons to Jesus.' He went on to describe two such cases of convincing conversion of mentally retarded people – clear illustrations that none are written off as 'unreachable' when the Spirit of God moves in revival power.

In 1860 the new Moderator of the Free Church of Scotland addressed the General Assembly in Edinburgh as follows, 'We, as a Church, accept the revival as a great and blessed fact. Numerous and explicit testimonies from ministers and members alike bespeak the gracious influence upon the people.' A feature of this visitation in Scotland was the widespread blessing; virtually the whole country was affected. The magazine *The Revival* in 1865 reported, 'It was a very blessed season, perhaps the most extensive in its operation that we have ever known among us.'

In England, as soon as news was received of the

awakening in America, little groups of 'prayer-warriors' sprang up everywhere. For example, in 1858 special prayer meetings for revival were started in Newcastle-on-Tyne and they continued for a year. Dr. and Mrs. Walter Palmer, who had been especially involved in the original outbreak of revival in the city of Hamilton, Ontario, Canada, in 1857, arrived in Newcastle in the late part of summer 1859. Their visit brought the first stirrings of blessing. *The Times* (no less) reported, 'Newcastle has become the scene of a religious "Awakening" which bids fair to rival anything of the kind which has occurred either in America or the North of Ireland.'

When revival fully broke out it seemed, as in Scotland, to touch the whole land. London was visited in no uncertain way, and people were brought to Christ in droves. It does not seem that there were any prostrations or other such phenomena, but it was revival without doubt. Generally speaking the London revival of that period was one of powerful preaching. Spurgeon had already been preaching for five years in London with great crowds and much blessing, but even for 'the prince of preachers', 1859 was 'high water mark'. He wrote in 1860, 'The times of refreshing from the presence of the Lord have at last dawned upon our land. A spirit of prayer is visiting our churches. The first breath of the rushing mighty wind is already discerned, while on rising evangelists the tongues of fire have evidently descended.' The 'rising evangelists' to whom Spurgeon referred were Robert Aitken, William Haslam, Richard Weaver and Reginald Radcliffe, among many others of like calibre. The saintly and scholarly Bishop Handley Moule could never forget the revival which visited rural Dorset in 1859 when he was a very young man, 'Fordington was one of the scenes of Divine Awakening, for surely it was Divine. The simplest means carried with them a heavenly power. The plain reading of a chapter often conveyed the call of God to men and women, and they "came to Jesus as they were." ' He affirmed that hundreds of people were awakened and continued in grace.

A great social uplift resulted. Manchester, Liverpool, the Potteries, cities, towns, villages throughout the land cry out to be included in this chapter for 'honourable mention' of God's glory in revival, but space does not allow it.

At least a million people were converted in the United Kingdom in the 1859 Awakening. The full story has been told in detail and depth in Dr. J. Edwin Orr's matchless book *The Second Evangelical Awakening in Britain*.

The influence of the revival continued long after the high water mark of 1860, and the effects were world-wide, because this awakening revived all the existing missionary societies enabling them to enter other fields, and also brought new societies into being such as the China Inland Mission, founded by Hudson Taylor. The new missionary thrust was spear headed by persons revived or converted in the awakening. The various evangelistic and philanthropic organisations received a tremendous impetus on the home field, as well as new agencies such as the Salvation Army coming into being in the wake of the revival.

In those favoured years of 1857 to 1860 major revivals of a similar pattern were reported in Sweden and Norway (where a sober estimate is given of a quarter of a million converts in twelve months); with revival blessing also as far afield as Australia, Africa, the West Indies and India.

As a result of the revival, evangelism flourished for decades afterwards. Clearly there is no conflict between true revival and true evangelism. It is not 'revival or evangelism', but 'revival and evangelism'. The best and most faithful evangelism needs revival or the impact and the results will be small and shallow: the most glorious revival needs faithful evangelistic preaching and wise soul-winning efforts, otherwise even the greatest revivals produce much reduced abiding fruit.

In the words of E. J. Poole-Connor, 'It is God's normal order in times of revival to work through the preaching of the gospel. No proclamation which is not based upon the Scriptures as the veritable Word of God, the Deity of Christ, His atoning death, the necessity of regeneration through personal faith in the Saviour, has ever been acknowledged by Him as the instrument of salvation.'

9

Wales 1904

'Bend the church and save the world . . .' cried a young Welsh mine worker, with all the passion of his prayer-burdened heart; and God did. Within a year more than one hundred thousand people had been swept into the Kingdom of God.

The young Welshman in question, Evan Roberts, was born on 8th June, 1878, in the little Welsh town of Loughor, some eight miles from Swansea. Evan, in common with many other boys in the valleys, began work at an early age in a coal-mine. When he was older he took up the trade of a blacksmith in connection with the mines. From his early teen years the hand of God rested upon him. William Davies, a deacon at the Moriah Chapel which Evan attended, warned him not to miss the prayer meetings in case the Holy Spirit 'would come' and he would be missing, like Thomas who missed the first appearance of the Risen Saviour. For thirteen years Evan was always in the prayer meetings. At the age of twenty-six he felt the call of God to preach. Having had very little education he entered the preparatory school at Newcastle-Emlyn to prepare himself to enter Trevecca College. He entered the Newcastle-Emlyn grammar school in the autumn, just at the time in the providence of God when Seth Joshua, the successful Welsh evangelist, was holding special services some eight miles away at

Blaenanerch. Evan attended with his closest friend Sidney Evans and a group of other young people, on Thursday, 29th September, 1904.

Seth Joshua was born in the great revival year of 1859 and was converted twenty-three years later. In 1904 he was operating as the denominational evangelist of the Calvinistic Methodist Church. In the spring of the year he had encountered quite a lot of opposition which had driven him to God in prayer and study of the Word. He was afraid of the growing emphasis on intellectual qualifications for the ministry rather than spiritual attainments and he began to pray that God would take a lad from the mines or fields of Wales to revive His work. He little realised that the answer to that prayer was walking into his service at Blaenanerch on that Thursday evening.

It was a very powerful service and at the close Seth Joshua prayed, 'Bend us, O Lord . . .' Immediately the Spirit of God bore witness to young Evan, 'This is what you need.' Evan was gripped with the spirit of intercession. He himself recalled what happened, 'I fell on my knees with my arms over the seat in front of me and the tears flowed freely. I cried, "Bend me! Bend me! Bend me! Bend us!" Perspiration poured down my face and tears streamed quickly – until I thought that the blood came out. Soon Mrs. Davies came to wipe my perspiration away. When I was in this feeling the audience sang heartily, "I am coming, coming Lord to Thee!" Now a great burden came upon me for the salvation of lost souls.' He revealed later that what had overwhelmed him was a great sense of God's love and his own unworthiness. Evan always looked back upon that meeting as the vital turning point in his praying for revival; 'Blaenanerch's great meeting' he termed it.

Evan Roberts' bosom friend Sydney Evans was at the school along with him. One midnight after walking in the garden in communion with God, Evan Roberts went indoors, his face shining to the point of glowing. Young Sydney was astonished and asked, 'Evan, what has happened to you?' 'Oh, Syd,' he replied, 'I have got wonderful news for you. I had a vision of all Wales being lifted up to heaven. We are going to see the mightiest revival that Wales has ever known – and the Holy Spirit is coming just now. We must get ready. We must have a little band and go all over the country preaching.'

For many years revival had been the passion of his heart. He said, 'I could sit up all night to read or talk about revivals. It was the Spirit that moved me to think about revival.' At times he was overwhelmed by the presence of God. On occasions his body trembled until his bed was shaken. One night his brother Dan awoke and shouted, 'Are you ill, Evan?' The truth is that for weeks he enjoyed times of rare and intimate communion with God in the night watches, such as few are privileged to enjoy. All this was behind that prayer from his heart of 'Bend me!'

A month after that prayer, on the 31st October, Evan Roberts felt a strong leading from the Lord to return home from school to Loughor. In a letter of that date he wrote to a friend, 'Just to let you know that I am on my way home for a week to work with our young people. The reason for this is the command of the Holy Spirit.' Immediately on arriving home he told his mother and brother, 'There will be a great change in Loughor in less than a fortnight. We are going to have the greatest revival that Wales has ever seen.'

He went straight to his pastor and asked permission to hold services for young people. After the adult prayer meeting, just sixteen adults and one little girl remained behind at Evan's invitation. He quietly explained why he had come home and mentioned the promised revival. On Tuesday, 1st November, there were more present as he spoke on the importance of being filled with the Holy

Spirit. He laid great emphasis on the work of the Holy Spirit. In later years he wrote, 'The baptism of the Holy Spirit is the essence of revival, for revival comes from a knowledge of the Holy Spirit and the way of co-working with Him which enables Him to work in revival power. The primary condition of revival is therefore that believers should individually know the baptism of the Holy Ghost.'

The following night for the first time he spoke on the four great points which became such an important part of his message. 'Do you desire an outpouring of the Spirit? Very well, four conditions must be observed:

1. Is there any sin in your past that you have not confessed to God? On your knees at once. Your past must be put away and yourself cleansed.
2. Is there anything in your life that is doubtful? Have you forgiven everybody, everybody, EVERYBODY? If not, don't expect forgiveness for your own sins. You won't get it.
3. Do what the Spirit prompts you to do. Obedience – prompt, implicit, unquestioning obedience to the Spirit.
4. A public confession of Christ as your Saviour. There is a vast difference between profession and confession.'

Throughout the week the meetings continued; the atmosphere became warmer and the opposition to 'the young prophet' melted. He was invited to preach in the Sunday evening service and at the close of his message some sixty young people responded for salvation. Then he taught the people to pray, 'Send the Spirit now for Christ's sake.' It was after midnight before they dispersed.

The Monday prayer meeting next evening was packed out. Evan Roberts read the last chapter of Malachi and the people were astonished at his holy boldness as he emphasised that this blessed Scripture was going to be fulfilled right then in Loughor. Many were moved to tears, others cried in agony. This was the first time that the 'Revival Love Song' was first sung – 'Here is love, vast as the ocean . . .' The meeting did not close until 3 a.m.

Yet quite surprisingly on the next evening, Tuesday, 8th November, the atmosphere in the service was quite cold and Roberts agonised in prayer for God to melt the atmosphere with Christ's Calvary love. They were there until the early hours. But now the community was affected and at 6 a.m. on the Wednesday morning people were awakened by the sound of crowds flocking to the early morning prayer meeting. The whole town was rapidly becoming 'a prayer meeting.'

The next day he preached at Brynteg and the following night also, when for the first time the Press carried reports of the revival. *The Cardiff Western Mail* carried a short article headed, 'Great Crowds of People Drawn to Loughor.' It began, 'A remarkable religious revival is now taking place in Loughor . . . Dense crowds . . . unable to obtain admission. Shopkeepers are closing early to get a place in the chapel, and tin and steel workers throng the place in their working clothes.' After that the news of the revival was reported daily.

Prayer was the order of the day. Believers were burdened for the salvation of their loved ones. The one theme of conversation was the Lord Jesus Christ and His glorious triumphs. On Friday, 11th November Moriah Chapel was filled to overflowing again with some eight hundred people. On Saturday, prayer meetings were held in many homes in Loughor and in the afternoon people began to flock into the town from the outlying areas. The two chapels (Moriah and Pisgah) were crowded with Evan Roberts preaching in one and his friend Sydney Evans in the other.

On Sunday 13th Roberts was in Aberdare; it was a rather disappointing day but on Monday, Ebenezer Congregational Chapel, Aberdare, was crowded with a thousand people, and on Tuesday the whole neighourhood was stirred. People did not go to work but attended the early morning prayer meeting which lasted four hours. Immense crowds poured into the town and in the evening service, Evan Roberts announced a hymn which became one of the revival hymns: 'Heavenly Jesus, ride victorious, Gird Thy sword upon Thy thigh.' Praise and prayer broke out spontaneously. Roberts walked through the chapel clapping his hands in holy ecstasy. At a most intense moment in the service he proclaimed that a mighty revival was coming to ALL Wales and that they in Aberdare were only opening the gates for it. James A. Stewart, the Scottish evangelist was privileged to spend time with Evans Roberts' family, and in his intimate book about Evan Roberts and the revival, *Invasion of Wales by the Spirit through Evan Roberts* he says, 'By the end of these meetings the whole of Wales and Britain knew that the Holy Spirit had come to the Principality.'

From Aberdare, Evan Roberts moved around the towns up and down the valleys of South Wales.

The presence of God was felt everywhere. The atmosphere was divinely charged. A miner who was converted in the revival once described it in the following graphic way. He said that he had been in the revival and he had also on one occasion been in an underground explosion in one of the local pits and there was not much to choose between the two! The atmosphere underground was charged with dust and methane gas, and the atmosphere in Wales in the revival was impregnated with the presence of God. For a vital period young Evan Roberts was the central human figure in the awakening and no-one who studies it in depth will ever want to minimise the important part he played or denigrate him as a person in any way – he was 'a divinely chosen vessel'; but he was not the only one, neither in its commencement nor in its continuance did the revival only centre on him.

In the August Welsh Keswick Week of 1904 at Llandrindod Wells, the Spirit of God broke forth in power as F. B. Meyer ministered. In that same month the renowned evangelist Reuben A. Torrey had a mission in Cardiff with a great ingathering of souls. For a year before that there had been a prayer meeting in Penarth from 6 a.m to 7 a.m. Torrey reported, 'For the first two weeks things dragged. Then we appointed a day of fasting and prayer and the day was observed in other parts of Wales. In one place Seth Joshua wrote me a glowing account of what God had done on that day. I think it was on that very day that he was kneeling beside Evan Roberts and the power of God fell upon him. The power of God came down in Cardiff too. When we left, the meeting went right on without us and they went on for a whole year – meetings every night and multitudes converted.' James A. Stewart estimates that there were at least forty thousand earnest believers seeking God in prayer for revival before 1904.

By the time 1905 dawned the revival was really under way and throughout that year there was no stopping it. For two glorious years the Welsh churches were crowded out. 'A hundred thousand outsiders were converted and added to the churches, the vast majority remaining true to the end' says Edwin Orr in *The Re-Study of Revival and Revivalism*.

The whole of Wales was now affected. Hardened unbelievers were gloriously converted. Drunkards, thieves, gamblers were transformed. Confessions of awful sins were heard on every side. Old debts were paid. Miners prayed together before commencing their shifts in the coal-mines. Pit ponies unused to the new kindness and clean language, without the usual kicks and curses, almost stopped work until they got adjusted. Courts had few cases to try. Whole football and rugby teams got converted and fixtures were abandoned. The young men were more concerned with praying than playing! Dance halls were deserted, the pubs were empty and not a few went out of business, but the prayer meetings were crowded.

David Matthews in his eye-witness account, *I Saw the Welsh Revival*, describes the services, 'Such marvellous singing, quite extempore, could only be created by a supernatural power – the Holy Spirit. No choir, no conductor, no organ – just spontaneous, unctionised soul-singing. Once the first hymn was given out, the meeting conducted itself. There was no leader, but people felt an unseen control. Singing, sobbing, praying intermingled and proceeded without intermission.'

Great men of God visited Wales and declared the work to be of God. As in every revival there were some extravagances, some fanaticism, but the main work was glorious with lasting results. Those who would glibly dismiss it as 'mere emotionalism' and 'just singing and praying, no preaching, no lasting results,' have been proved to have been absolutely wrong by those who have taken the time and trouble to carefully research the aftermath of the 1904 Revival, most notable of such researchers being Edwin Orr. He has proved conclusively that the Welsh Revival, far from being confined to Wales, 'was the farthest-reaching of all the movements of the Awakening, for it affected the whole evangelical cause in India, Korea and China, renewed revivals in Japan and South Africa, and sent a wave of awakening over Africa, Latin America and the South Seas.' (Edwin Orr). The rest of Britain was also affected, the Awakening of 1905 'affected each of the counties of England'; the happenings may not have been quite as explosive as those in Wales but they were extraordinary nevertheless. The springs of the Pentecostal Movement in Wales and beyond can also be traced back to the Welsh Revival of 1904; such great Pentecostal evangelists as Stephen and

George Jeffreys were raised up in the years which followed, not to mention such time-honoured servants of God as John Thomas and John Daniel Jones and a host of others with world-affecting ministries, who were very much the 'children of the revival.'

As James A. Stewart says, 'Bend the Church and save the world,' is the secret of every true awakening. Here is part of a prayer that Evan Roberts prayed in one of the great revival meetings in one of the towns where over thirteen hundred new converts were rejoicing in their new found faith, 'Lord Jesus, help us now through the Holy Spirit to come face to face with the cross. Whatever the hindrances may be, we commit the service to Thee. Put us all under the blood. Oh, Lord, place the blood on all our past up to this moment. We thank Thee for the blood. In the name of Jesus Christ, bind the devil this moment. We point to the cross of Christ. Oh, open the heavens. Descend upon us now. We shall give all the glory to Thy Name. No one else has a right to the glory but Thee – take it, Lord. Glorify Thy Son in this meeting. Oh, Holy Spirit, do Thy work through us and in us now. Speak Thy word in power for Thy Name's sake. Amen – and Amen!'

10

The Latin American Explosion

'Brazil is a land where the greatest national revival of the twentieth century is now in force,' says Steve Durasoff in *Bright Wind of the Spirit*. Church Growth specialist, Peter Wagner, says 'The Protestant Church is increasing at a rate three times that of the population in general. In 1900 there were about 50,000 Protestants in Latin America. In the 1930s growth passed the one million mark. In the 1940s it passed the two million mark. In the 1950s it passed the five million mark. In the 1960s it passed the 10 million mark. In the 1970s it zoomed past the 20 million mark. Some statisticians project something around 100 million for 2000 AD.' (*Look Out the Pentecostals are Coming*.)

Brazil, with a population around 120 million occupies half of the South American continent. This great and developing country has been experiencing almost continuous revival for over seventy years, and there is no sign of abatement – rather the very opposite. When Dr. Billy Graham visited Brazil he was asked if he knew the secret of the growth of the work of God there. He replied, 'Every Pentecostal believer is a preacher.' The commencement of the Pentecostal work in Brazil is one of the great romances of Pentecostal missionary work. In

1910 two Swedish immigrants to America, Daniel Berg and Gunnar Vingren, were called by God to leave Chicago and commence a missionary work in Para, Brazil. They were in a small prayer meeting in South Bend, Indiana, when a prophecy was given to them telling them to 'go to Para.' Para? They had never heard of it. Searching in the public library they discovered that it was a state in Brazil.

Whilst they were still wondering how they would get there, another prophecy instructed them to go to New York and there look for a certain man at a certain place. Talk about Philip going into the desert! Their available money was just enough to get them on the night train to New York. There they did indeed find the man and he provided them with the exact fare to Belem, the capital of Para. 'They arrived in Brazil, bewildered and exhausted,' says Peter Wagner. 'Their wool suits were hardly appropriate attire for one of the world's hottest tropical cities. They sat on a park bench, not knowing what to do next, but praying for God to guide them. He guided them first to a Methodist missionary, who introduced them to a friendly Baptist pastor who in turn provided them with lodging in some rooms behind the church.'

Their red-hot message of Holy Ghost power, however, proved rather too much for their new-found friends and soon they formed their own church. From the first, God worked with them in revival power and blessing. Today the proof that they were truly called of God is that the work they started is now the largest Protestant work in all Latin America. Daniel Berg died in 1963 in his eightieth year, a highly respected leader; his companion Gunner Vingren preceded him in his home-call by a few years; but the work they founded, Assemblies of God in Brazil, is still moving forward in revival power with some ten million members and adherents.

At the beginning of the twentieth century, a pioneer Methodist minister, T. B. Wood, made this prophetic statement: 'The signs of the times point to the coming of great sweeping revivals. All the work thus far is providentially preparatory to them. And when they once get started . . . the mighty changes that will follow . . . promise to surpass anything of the kind hitherto known.'

In 1951 there were signs of an awakening in Brazil among some of the historic Protestant churches. Edwin Orr has not only written extensively on revivals but has also been used of God on several occasions as His instrument in revival. In 1951 he paid a hurried visit to Brazil, and at short notice, Professor Walter Ermel arranged for him to address the students in the Faculty of Theology in São Paulo. The Professor himself testified to being wonderfully blessed. He said, 'At the last meeting I had an experience of victory over sins which until then I had been unable to conquer. The students of the Seminary were also revived spiritually and began morning prayer meetings for revival in Brazil.' Springing out of that visit, a prayer movement began with eighty churches in the city praying weekly for revival.

Many of them were praying that God would send Edwin Orr back to Brazil for a longer visit, which transpired the following year in 1952. The meetings were supported by all denominations and a general awakening followed, which, according to the evangelical church council, was the first of such a general nature in their history. Many of the theological colleges were affected by this visitation. In the return visit to the Seminary in São Paulo in March, the Spirit of God began to work and many came to the place of penitence and prayer. Edwin Orr stayed eleven weeks in that great city. God gave him a wonderful interpreter which was absolutely vital. The story behind this provision was remarkable. In 1930, an American visitor to Brazil had spoken about revival in such a way that the wife of a high government official in the Federal Commission of Immigration went forward to seek prayer. Dr. Lima's wife, Dona Else Lima, then impulsively placed her infant daughter in the arms of the missionary and asked him to pray that the baby girl would be used of God in the reviving of the work of God in Brazil. In 1952 the daughter, Silvia Lima, had returned from academic success in America but having lost out spiritually. She was visiting São Paulo and out of curiosity she went to one of the packed-out meetings where Edwin Orr's interpreter had failed to turn up because of illness. Edwin Orr prevailed upon this brilliant but reluctant young lady to help him out. She was an immediate success; even more important, she was renewed spiritually and joined the Orr team for ministry throughout Brazil.

Edwin Orr visited each of the twenty-five states and territories of Brazil, which was a mammoth undertaking. Everywhere the Spirit of God moved again and again the largest auditoriums could not hold the great crowds. The British and Foreign Bible Society reported, 'Brazil is being shaken by the winds of the Spirit as never before.' Thousands came to Christ as Saviour and Lord. The churches were crowded for prayer at 6 o'clock in the morning; and evening meetings had to be transferred from the largest churches to soccer stadiums. Some churches increased by fifty per cent in a week. The upsurge continued for the next ten years, and many were called to the ministry and mission fields.

One of the most noteworthy churches in Brazil today is the Brazil for Christ Church in São Paulo, led by Manoel de Melo, who is one of the most outstanding Pentecostal leaders in South America and is known and respected around the world. He is a great man with a simple faith and a gentle humility which enables God to use him in remarkable ways. Under his leadership his church has recently completed a vast sanctuary which will seat 25,000 people. The Brazil for Christ nationwide has over 4,000 churches; they are planting churches and winning people to Christ all the time. As Peter Wagner says, 'The basic dynamic behind Pentecostal growth in Latin America is the power of the Holy Spirit.' It is generally accepted that some 80 per cent of Protestants in Brazil are Pentecostals.

Brazil, however, is just a part of the Latin American revival story. Argentina has witnessed episodes worthy of the Acts of the Apostles. As in Brazil, the Pentecostal work was started by two humble, 'unknown' believers. They were Italians, newly-filled with the Spirit of God, who at the call of God went from Chicago to Buenos Aires and arrived unheralded. From that humble beginning there are now hundreds of Christian assemblies in various parts of Argentina. Other missionaries followed and laboured faithfully but for the most part for many years the results were quite small. In the 1950s many of the missionaries were feeling down-hearted. Much of their labour seemed to have been in vain. They needed a breath of revival and they prayed, but discouragement deepened for nothing seemed to be happening.

God, however, was at work answering their prayers in His own mysterious and wonderful ways. In 1952 in Tallahassee, Florida, a forty-four year old evangelist, Tommy Hicks, was in prayer when God gave him a vision of a map of South America. The map was covered with a vast field of yellow grain, ready for harvest. It was a clear Macedonian call. As he prayed the grain changed to men and women with uplifted hands crying, 'Come, Brother Hicks, come and help us!' As he continued to pray God gave him a message which he wrote in his Bible: 'For two snows will not pass over the earth until thou shalt go to this land, for thou shalt not go by boat nor by land but as a bird, flying through the air shalt thou go.' Hicks kept the vision to himself and the message. But three months later in California in a pastor's home, during prayer the pastor's wife stretched out her hand and repeated the identical message.

Tommy Hicks began to prepare for the journey, knowing virtually nothing about Argentina. God provided funds for a one-way ticket to Buenos Aires. During the last part of the flight the name 'Peron' kept coming to his mind. He felt sure God was speaking but the name meant nothing to him, so he asked the stewardess who told him, 'Mr. Peron is the President of Argentina.' Hicks took it that God wanted him to talk to the President, so he sought an interview with him. All the missionaries warned him against even trying; Peron was a dictator and freedom was limited. It could be dangerous. Hicks, however, would not be deterred. He presented himself at the office of the Minister of Religion – 'No, Peron would not see him.' Then the Minister's secretary came in limping, his left leg was stiffened and black. Hicks suggested they prayed about it and the secretary scoffed that even Christ himself couldn't help this leg! Nevertheless, Hicks prayed and God worked a miracle. The astonished and delighted secretary forthwith promised to take Hicks to see Peron. The way having been so marvellously prepared, Peron was more than responsive and gave instructions for every help to be given to him.

Hicks was given the use of a large stadium and free access to government radio and press. The crusade had a far reaching effect. Peter Wagner says, 'Recent studies on the church in Argentina have revealed the crucial importance of the Tommy Hicks' campaign of 1954, not only for the Pentecostals, but also for all other churches which co-operated.' Arno Enns, who has written the standard church history of Argentina, calls the Hicks campaign 'a sovereign breakthrough of God.' The influential book, *Latin American Church Growth* says, 'Many Evangelicals in Argentina, whether or not they agree with Hicks's theology, admit that his meetings broke the back of the rigid Argentine resistance to the evangelical witness.'

He preached for fifty-two days to an aggregate attendance of some two million, with an accepted figure of some 200,000 in the final meeting. Researchers seem satisfied that a figure of something approaching 20,000 converts is right, which was the greatest gain ever in Argentina. All Evangelicals profited, but the Pentecostals particularly began a period of rapid growth, which is still continuing in the 1980s.

Chile is another Latin American country which has experienced revival in this present century. There was an outpouring of the Holy Spirit at the Methodist Episcopal Church in Valparaiso in 1909 when the congregation grew very quickly from 150 to more than 900. The pastor was an American missionary, Willis C. Hoover, who had been praying for revival. Before he had gone to the mission field he had been in a church in Chicago which had experienced something of the power of revival in 1895. The longing in his heart for God to do something similar in his church in Valparaiso increased. He wanted God to visit them with the same power that was so clearly promised in the Acts of the Apostles. The city of Valparaiso was counted by some as one of the world's most wicked cities, and when it was wrecked by an earthquake in 1906 there were those who said it was a judgement. In 1907, Hoover's wife received a letter and a tract from a former classmate of her Chicago days, Minnie Abrams, who was then working in India with the internationally known Pandita Ramabai. Minnie told them of the outpouring of God's Spirit upon the girls in the school there which had been accompanied with speaking in tongues, visions, great conviction and true revival power. The news inspired them to fresh seeking of God in prayer. A member of the congregation was a night watchman and on the morning of January 14, 1909, he was back at home in bed in a deep sleep when Christ appeared to him in a vivid dream. It was a new experience for him as a Methodist. In the dream the Lord Jesus told him to go and tell his pastor to gather the praying members of his church and to pray together daily because 'I intend to baptise them with tongues of fire.' The man was obedient and immediately went and shared his dream with Willis Hoover who accepted the dream as a revelation and confirmation from God of what he had been praying about for months.

They started their daily prayer meetings and very soon they began to experience unusual happenings. Believers were renewed as they confessed their hidden sins. Hardened pagans were converted. Others received visions and dreams and their faith began to rise. By April 1909, the revival was a reality. By October, the congregation had grown to nine hundred (from one hundred and fifty) and the blessing was spreading to other congregations, but they now began to encounter bitter opposition over various manifestations, especially tongues, healing, prophecies, prostrations and visions. The Annual Conference of the Methodist Church in Chile finally 'resolved to eliminate the pastor from the work by sending him home.' On learning this, some eighteen members of the official board, with some four hundred others, resolved to separate from the Methodist Episcopal Church and under Willis Hoover, the Methodist Pentecostal Church in Chile was founded. Donald Gee reported that by 1932, 'the total membership of that church was over 10,000 and it was constantly growing.' Today the membership is around the million mark, which compares with the 4,000 in the Methodist Church that did not have place for such working of the Holy Spirit back in 1909 and 1910. David Coombs in *The Flame Still Spreads* says that '80 per cent of evangelicals in Chile are Pentecostal.'

Revival always brings a renewed faith in the person and power of the Holy Spirit of God. This is so clearly revealed in these words of Willis Hoover, 'I believe that the true secret of this whole thing is that we really and truly believe in the Holy Spirit – we really trust Him – we really honour Him – we really obey Him – we really give Him free rein – we really believe that the promise in Acts 1:4–5 and Joel 2:28–29 is for us.'

Dramatic movements of the Spirit of God have also been witnessed in Ecuador, Columbia, Peru, Bolivia and in the Amazon Valley. Missionaries, after years of getting nowhere, have suddenly been able to report movings of the Holy Spirit the like of which they have never seen before. Many of them freely confess that they cannot explain it and they can only say in amazed wonder, 'The Spirit works as He wills. There is no other explanation.'

11

The Long Arm of Armenian Destiny

Armenia, 'this oldest Christian nation is also the one which has suffered most for its faith,' write John and Elizabeth Sherrill. This small embattled country, which is now one of the Soviet republics, has been the scene of both revival and suffering in the twentieth century. The Armenians endured savagery and persecution on a scale that provided Hitler with his blue-print for the extermination of the Jews. A revival at the beginning of the century which centred on Tarsus – the birth-place of the Apostle Paul – prepared them for the holocaust to come. Their story is one of the most heart-rending and moving and must rank with any of the terrible periods of the suffering but triumphant Church.

One who shared in that revival was Rev. Sisag Manoogian who eventually became the President of the Armenian Evangelical Union. In his biography *Out of the Ark*, his daughter (Mrs. Rhoda Carswell) wrote 'The years 1900–1901 are remembered amongst the Armenians living in S.E. Turkey as the years of the great religious revival. The revival appears to have started in the Aintab area and spread to all the Armenian areas along the south-east coast. The minister of the Tarsus Armenian Church was in Aintab at the time of the revival, and he returned home full of the Spirit and greatly changed by what he had witnessed. Prayer became the dominant feature of his life, and he would pray without ceasing.'

It was not long before he was seeing the answers to his prayers. 'Many were won over to the Lord, including a number of prominent personalities,' wrote Mrs. Carswell. 'My father, too, was born again. He and three other young men from Tarsus went to Adana and testified there of the changes that had been worked by God in their lives, and it was not long before Adana and Tarsus were agog. The church was really alive. Services continued until midnight and the churches were unable to hold all who wanted to attend. In the market place and wherever people gathered, conversation centred on 'the revival'. Prayer, confession and testimony were the order of the day, and father looked back throughout his life to this period as a blessed time. Some of the young people converted at this time were amongst the roughest and crudest of the youth in the town. They became true believers and a means of blessing not only to the church but also to the town.'

Many of those newly awakened souls were soon destined to die in one of the most terrible massacres of all time. As Hitler later noted, 'The world did not intervene when Turkey wiped out the Armenians.' Lord Bryce estimated that out of 4¼ million Armenians alive in 1914, less than 2 million were still living in 1918. His chronicle of the mass murders of the Armenians by the Turks, *The Treatment of the Armenians in the Ottoman Empire*, was presented to Lord Grey, the British Foreign Secretary in 1916. In it he estimated that in 1915 alone, 800,000 Armenians were brutally and systematically slaughtered by the Turks, among them a vast host of Armenian Christians.

In the first World War, Turkey was allied to Germany. Over many years the Turks had tried to exterminate the Armenians, who held the distinction of being the first

country to officially embrace Christianity – way back in
the time of the Roman Empire. The Turkish Islam tradition and the Armenian Christian faith were long in conflict. 1915 afforded Turkey its pretext for annihilation.
In fighting between the Russians and Turks on the
Caucasian front, a number of Armenians fighting with
the Russians were captured. This was not surprising
because Russia had annexed part of Turkish Armenia
forty years earlier. Immediately all Armenians living in
Turkey were 'suspect'. The order was given that Armenians were plotting insurrection and all were to be
rounded up and either put to death or deported to the
desert wastes in Syria and beyond, and so it was that
the massacre began.

Talking about those terrible times, a member of an
exiled Armenian family – Demos Shakarian said, 'They
would herd those Armenians into barns a thousand at a
time, put straw around it and light a match. Before they
would light the match they would ask if there was anyone
who would deny Christ and accept Mohammed; but they
did not deny Christ, they were willing to die for Him.'

Murder, outrage and torture were the key words in the
authenticated report gathered together by Lord Bryce,
'About one and a half million people in August 1915
were driven into the deserts of Mesopotamia. Routes
through the desert and the waters of the River Euphrates
were strewn with corpses. Many people have been
beaten to death.'

Some of the happenings were devilish and horrible in
the extreme. Babies became the playthings for the guards
to toss from one to another to catch on bayonet ends, or
to hurl them down the precipice. Guards taunted their
captives. A Syrian pastor in Ourfa saw thousands of
Armenian women and children on one of these 'desert
marches.' He said that nearly all were hungry, thirsty,
and literally naked. Yet, in spite of all their sufferings,
some of them found pieces of charcoal and wrote on the

rocks a few lines to encourage those following behind: 'As Jesus did not deny us, do not deny Him. We have not denied Him. Follow us.'

Armenian orphans knelt in their orphanages and prayed that the faith of their mothers and sisters, who had been snatched from them by Kurds and Turks on the desert marches, might be strong till death. There were the inevitable rapes, after which many girls were impaled on swords. Djevet Bey, the Governor of one province, earned the title of 'The Blacksmith'. His favourite torture was to have horse shoes nailed to men's feet, in attempts to get them to confess to hiding or possessing arms. Little wonder that a famous London preacher when learning of such atrocities in previous Turkish slaughters of the Armenians, had been provoked to exclaim from his pulpit 'God damn the Sultan. . .' But the response of these Armenians was different. In a tract he published in 1921, *Armenian Experts in the Art of Dying*, Rev. Manoogian wrote 'Instead of begging for mercy, they showed calm and dignity; instead of cursing, they prayed for forgiveness for their murderers. In their defencelessness they tried to defend the weaker ones; in their hunger they shared their last piece of bread with the poorest.'

Fortunately for the Christian Church some of these amazing Armenian Christians have been spared to bless the world today. Their survival in many cases is directly linked to revival. The Rev. Manoogian in a letter to his mother-in-law in 1916 wrote, 'The Lord rescued me from death on thirty different occasions.' Many of his escapes were as exciting and fantastic as that of Saul of Tarsus from Damascus in a basket (I Cor 11:32,33).

Revivals produce Christians of a very special calibre. Another Armenian family which was spared to bless millions is the Shakarian family. This family were Presbyterians who lived in the Armenian town of Kara Kala, situated on the rocky foothills of Mount Ararat. In the

1850s there were great outpourings of the Holy Spirit upon hundreds of thousands of Russian Orthodox Christians. From time to time caravans of these revived Russians went down into Armenia to share the blessings of revival. But as respectable Presbyterians the Shakarian family found the Russians' stories of miracles and healings and tongues too 'way out' for them. The Russians made much of the 'anointing of the Holy Spirit.' When the Spirit of God came upon them they would raise their arms and dance with joy. But eventually, after many years of arguing and resisting, Mr. Shakarian was broken by an undeniable manifestation of God's power – when a secret known only to himself was startlingly revealed by one of these Russian 'prophets'. Completely broken, Mr. Shakarian knelt before one of the Russian leaders and in tears he said, 'Show me how I can receive the Spirit of God.' He knelt and an old Russian laid his hands on his head. Immediately Mr. Shakarian burst into joyous prayer in a language neither he nor anyone present could understand. The Russians called this kind of ecstatic utterance 'tongues' and regarded it as a sign that the Holy Spirit was present with the speaker. Mrs. Shakarian likewise received the Spirit the same night in 1900 – before the present Pentecostal Movement was heard of.

By a great miracle the Shakarian family and other Christian families from their area left before the massacres. Some of the Russian revivalists had settled in Kara Kala in the 1850s, including the Klubniken family. Their son, Efim, was only eleven but already mighty in prayer. One day the Spirit of God moved this boy to pray and fast for a week. As he sat in his little home God gave him a vision of charts and a message in beautiful handwriting. That was in 1855. Mr. Shakarian's grandson, Demos, now a millionaire dairy farmer in America, retold the story, 'Although Efim was an illiterate boy, he wrote in beautiful handwriting and drew pictures, maps and charts. He foretold that peace would be taken from the earth and that Armenia would be overrun by the Turks and that the Armenian Christians would be massacred unless they went to a land across the ocean. Those charts pointed to America. When my father was born, Efim was still living in that community. He was then a man past fifty years of age, but he was still walking with God. Then one day he prophesied again, 'The time has come. You Armenian people must leave. Destruction is coming.' Those Christians who did not believe that God speaks today to people in this way, thought this was foolishness. They laughed at those who left for America, just the way they laughed at Noah in the Bible. By 1905 our family finally sailed for America. By 1915 the very same place where I was born was wiped out.'

Today, Demos Shakarian and other Armenian exiled families who obeyed this warning, are being mightily used of God. Demos especially has been used of God in revival blessing among businessmen across America and in many parts of the world. 'The Full Gospel Business Men's Fellowship International,' which he founded has been amazingly successful in winning businessmen for Christ. The full story has been graphically told in *The Happiest People on Earth*, as told by Demos Shakarian to John and Elizabeth Sherrill.

The Rev. Manoogian, when he thought his life was in danger in 1916, covenanted with God 'that if their baby son Peter lived (then just eighteen months old), he would work as a missionary among Moslems.' Peter Manoogian in due time became a missionary doctor working among Moslems in Lebanon, in the very areas where thousands of Armenians were killed in those terrible desert marches.

Sisag Manoogian wrote in 1921, 'The Armenians still have hope in the hopeless Turks. Our experts steadily look for a time in which Turkey shall be illumined with Turkish pastors and preachers of the Gospel. Then the world shall understand that God, the Greatest Economist, had graciously used even the blood of Armenians as "the seed of the church" to acomplish what the Armenian life had failed to do.'

God's ways are past finding out. Whoever could imagine anyone thanking God for an earthquake? Yet that is exactly what the Armenian Christians said after the terrible earthquake of 1988 had devastated a large part of their country. They said to John Wildrianne, a personal friend of mine who was among the first on the scene with relief from Christians in the west, 'We thank God for sending the earthquake because it has brought revival to Armenia'. John Wildrianne, in co-operation with Pentecostal Christians throughout Europe, was able to organise the building of a Pentecostal village in one of the worst hit areas. Prefabricated buildings were transported from Sweden and speedily erected, to shelter families living in tents from the freezing cold of the Armenian winter. When John Wildrianne asked them what more he could do for them in the way of relief, what was their top priority – was it clothes, food or money? They replied, 'What we need most is Bibles to share with our non-Christian friends so that we can win them for Christ'! That is revival – when the spiritual comes before the material.

The interpreter who was assigned to John Wildrianne's group of relief organisers was very quick to tell them that she was an atheist. However, on their return visit a few months later, this same interpreter met them and her first words were: 'I have become a Christian.' They soon experienced the depth of change which had taken place in her. The Swedish leader in the party had discovered that he had cancer and had been given only a few months to live, but had opted to make the trip. When the interpreter discovered this she immediately said, 'We must pray for you'. She took him into a church and prayed for his recovery in the name of Jesus. The Swedish leader recovered and God confirmed his word there in Armenia. That is what happens in times of revival.

12

Africa – God's Wind of Change

The rate of Christian growth in Africa since 1910 has been twice that of population growth, according to David Barrett. Thanks to the many Holy Spirit-inspired awakenings across this great continent, Bishop Stephen Neill is able to affirm on the most sober estimate that by the end of the twentieth century, Africa south of the Sahara will be in the main Christian.

Patrick Johnstone, author of the unique *Operation World*, believes there is a link between persecution and revival, 'The Holy Spirit seems to have anticipated in many places where persecution will come and has prepared His people for that by revival. For instance, this is true of East Africa, with Uganda and with the Mau Mau in Kenya – the revival came before. On the other hand it seems that revival and persecution go together. This is happening in Angola and in other countries in Africa. In Ethiopia this is also true today.'

Len Moules, the well known missionary statesman said, 'Africa was only 2 per cent Christian in 1902. By the end of this century Africa will be 45 per cent Christian, and is already the contender for the foremost Christian continent.' Christianity is winning the four-cornered contest for the soul of Africa; its three rivals, animism,

Islam, and atheistic communism, are proving no match for the Gospel of Christ proclaimed in the power of the Spirit of God. Almost every country across this vast African continent has its fascinating quota of revival stories; all clamour for inclusion, but a few 'samplers' will have to suffice.

Take Zaire (formerly Belgian Congo), deep in the heart of Africa. The Church there had been built up through such God-anointed pioneers as Livingstone; Stanley; Baptist, George Grenfell; Methodist Revivalist, William Taylor; Brethren, F. S. Arnot; C. T. Studd of W. E. C.; and W. F. P. Burton and James Salter of the Zaire Evangelistic Mission. Then in 1960 in the bloodbath which quickly followed the granting of Independence on the 30th June, the Congolese Church faced her fiery ordeal. No less than thirty-one evangelical missionaries were martyred in Zaire between 1960 and 1965, as well as hundreds of the most devoted Congolese pastors and leaders and thousands of their members.

By October 1960, the newly formed state of Zaire was in the grip of Communist and pagan insurgents who had been training and planning their rebellion for years. Fighting was widespread. One great Congolese Chief in the Kikondja area was murdered in cold blood and hacked to pieces along with several of his councillors. His Christian wife, her sister, his mother and several children, were killed with them. Corpses strewed the area for miles around. People were impaled on stakes. Rebel leaders wore two real dried human hands, one white and one black, and their badge proclaimed 'no mercy.'

A large section of the population between the ages of 10 and 60 was blotted out. Cannibalism was reintroduced with every other vile custom and superstition. Human flesh was sold openly on Stanleyville market. The old men declared that they had never seen such abandonment to vice, lust and drunkenness even in the worst days of heathenism. Missionaries who risked their lives to revisit parts of the country found that whole congregations had been obliterated. Men, women and children had been driven into one church, the thatch set alight, and they had been burned to cinders. All that remained was the ruined foundation of the church building and a collection of charred bones. Thousands of Christians fled into the forests and just how many died of starvation and exposure will never be known.

A veteran missionary of the Zaire Evangelistic Mission, Harold Womersley, said, 'The blow that fell in 1960 was the greatest since the inception of the Mission in 1915. A threatened annihilation of the Church. Pastors, elders, missionaries were senselessly slaughtered, churches burned down, whole congregations hacked to pieces while worshipping, blood running like water. It looked as though the church was finished.' But the gates of hell could not prevail against a Church that was built upon the Rock. The Great Unseen Head of the Church had been preparing His people by revival in readiness for their fiery trial. Between 1946 and 1949 Harold Womersley tells that there was 'a Divine visitation that happened suddenly in many far removed places all over the area of the Zaire Evangelistic Mission. (A region bigger than Britain). It spread over the whole of our Z.E.M. field. The awakening came after much prayer and fasting, days of prayer and fasting being regular. Remarkable visions occurred. Older people among the unsaved who could not read the Word were granted visions, often of heaven and hell. They immediately repented and believed and became great witnesses for Christ. Such events shook the community and brought in witch doctors who burnt their charms.'

The wave of revival blessing ensured that the Church was spiritually prepared to face the onslaught of evil. Throughout the remarkable history of the Mission there had been great evidence of the supernatural power of the Holy Spirit, so necessary to combat the centuries of

116

entrenched evil darkness. Harold Womersley, widely known as a person of the highest integrity and a most reliable and sober witness, testifies that on occasions there were 'manifestations of light or fire that anybody passing by could see.' A revived church is indestructible. After months of waiting and wondering just how the believers were faring, missionaries who had been forced to evacuate to South Africa or other neighbouring countries, heard reassuring trickles of news. The Congolese Christians were hungry, naked, destitute, but still believing, still standing firm in their faith. They were praying ceaselessly in their refuges in the forests and in caves. Their first request was for Bibles, not food!

As the troubles subsided there was an extraordinary revival. More than one rebel said, 'The more we kill these Christians the more they multiply. They have got a power we haven't got.' Disillusioned with politics, there was a sudden wholesale turning to God among the people. A Congolese pastor revealed, 'During the long period when we were cut off from the missionaries we had a remarkable visitation of the Spirit of God. The pastors of our district had been fasting and praying because of the bloodshed and persecution. As we were praying the Spirit descended on us in a wonderful way and His gifts operated among us. He told us many things in prophecy which have all come true. The Holy Spirit began to convict of sin as we went back to our churches to preach, and streams of men and women believed on the Lord Jesus and confessed their sins exactly as in Acts 19:17–20, bringing their heathen charms. This revival lasted eight months.' This was repeated throughout the great area of the Z.E.M.; revival broke out everywhere and thousands upon thousands were converted and added to the churches.

The secret behind the revival, says Harold Womersley, was, 'Intense prayer in Zaire and many other lands which drew down the refreshing showers of Holy Ghost blessing and the Word of God prevailed as in the Acts of the Apostles.' By 1965 the number of believers in the work of the Z.E.M. had doubled since Independence to 70,000, in some 1,200 churches. By 1975 the number of believers had doubled again to 145,000 with 2,400 churches. The work still continues in an exceptional wave of blessing with packed churches, regular conversions and wonderful healings and other 'signs and wonders'. In 1984 the number of churches was almost 3,000 with a corresponding increase in believers. And it must be made clear that the revival experienced by the Z.E.M. field was duplicated in other areas by evangelical missions such as the W.E.C. field (pioneered by C. T. Studd), and the Brethren field (pioneered by such godly men as F. S. Arnot and Dan 'Thinking Black' Crawford).

To the east of Zaire is the neighbouring country of Ruanda, which is forever assured a place of honour in the annals of revival for the East African Revival which broke out there in 1935 during famine conditions. Within a year it was sweeping Ruanda and Burundi and touching Uganda, Kenya and Tanganyika. Though mainly Anglican it also spread to other denominations. Two of the earliest leaders in this move were Dr. Joe Church and his African colleague, Simeoni Nsibambi. The spread of that revival has been told many times: one of the most recent books *Hill Ablaze* by Canon Bill Butler was published in 1976. As a member of the East African Revival Team he relates how these revived believers were nicknamed 'balokole' – 'The saved ones.' Their shining faces singled them out. They were too much for many cold Christians, and Canon Butler tells how twenty-five of these revived students were actually expelled from the Bishop Tucker Theological College for refusing to stop their 4 a.m. prayer meetings. In spite of their ill-treatment, the revived ones stayed in their churches and ultimately their true worth was recognised. The principal emphasis of the revival was on repentance. Under the purging flame of the Holy Spirit, Christians were melted and broken before God, resulting in a renewal of zeal and deeper fellowship between believers.

The spread of the revival to Uganda is undoubtedly one of the secrets behind the survival of the suffering Ugandan Church under the terrible regime of Idi Amin after his coup in 1971. Festo Kivengere relates the impact that the revival made upon him, 'Revival came first to our rather dead church in Kigezi District when I was a schoolboy in Kabale in 1935. We listened in amazement . . . never before had we seen such glowing faces. Almost no one responded during these meetings. We were too unfamiliar with the truth and scared by exposure to it. But during the next month many things happened. Schoolboys went to the headmaster, weeping, to return stolen books and to confess breaking the rules. Lives were changed all around us. People saw visions and dreamed dreams. So many repented that pagans were afraid to walk up our hill, for fear God would lay hold of them. The fire of God spread and congregations came alive spiritually.' And so it was that Idi Amin found that 'a revived church is indestructible.'

Bishop Festo Kivengere has told something of that story in his book written when he was in exile and before the removal of Amin, entitled *I Love Idi Amin*. Only a revived Christian could ever have conceived such a title. In it he reported that although thousands were dying for Christ, 'the exciting thing is that, in spite of this, young people and older ones are turning to the Lord during this new persecution, challenged and drawn by the testimony and lives of those who have died. A living church cannot be destroyed by fire or by guns.'

After the overthrow of the tyrant Idi Amin, the church has been playing a major role in the rebuilding of the ravaged nation of Uganda. In spite of Amin's intense persecution, the Christian community increased from 52 per cent to 65–70 per cent of the 12 million population.

An estimated 300,000 people were slaughtered during the eight years rule of Amin. When he returned from his exile, Bishop Kivengere said, 'Let there be no hate. Let there be no revenge. We will rebuild our nation on God's love.'

The years of rebuilding have been very difficult but the one feature that struck church leaders was 'the increased commitment of Christians, with many nominal Christians giving themselves fully to Christ.' As Bishop Kivengere says, 'A living church does not succumb because of pressure. The church becomes more a church when it is pressed on every side. In the words of Jesus, "the grain of wheat must fall into the ground and die." Life must die before it can multiply.'

In an article written shortly before his death on the 17th March, 1978, Len Moules said, 'one could almost use the term an "epidemic" of revivals. It is difficult to keep abreast of the reports of local stirrings of God and spiritual awakenings that are becoming nationwide in several countries.' In war-torn Ethiopia there were glorious reports of tremendous awakenings in the mountains of south-west Ethiopia, with results that rank with some of the greatest conversion movements in Africa's history. That was in 1978, and although the church has faced tremendous persecution by the Communist regime since then, there are reports of pockets of revival in 1983. And what shall we say of the awakenings in Ghana, and the current reports of revival in many parts of troubled Nigeria in 1983 and 1984, and Kenya and the revived Christians who survived the Mau Mau so that the church in Kenya today is growing by leaps and bounds? Africa is truly enjoying many revivals. Mention must be made of two of God's men in Africa today. The first is a Zulu, Nicholas B. H. Bhengu, and the second is a German, Reinhard W. G. Bonnke.

Nicholas Bhengu (called 'The Black Billy Graham' by *Time* magazine), was born in Zululand in 1909, the son of a Lutheran pastor. After a good schooling he ran away to Kimberley and joined the Communist party. He was converted in a Pentecostal church run by two young Americans and he severed his Communist connections. He went to the South Africa General Mission Bible School at Dumisa, Natal, where he completed his studies in 1936. He acknowledges his great debt to the school in the following testimony, 'I experienced the presence of the Lord in the classroom and the operation of the Holy Spirit as never before. It was there I learned of the amazing grace of God and His love that surpasses all understanding; there a passion for souls was born in my heart. Mr. Suter, our teacher, emphasised the need for messengers who would go at God's command without a salary. One day he said, "God wants a man." And I heard a still small voice say, "Nicholas, you are the man!" And I said, "God, I am that man." '

For a time he worked as a court interpreter which helped him to become proficient in English and Afrikaans; he also speaks perfect Zulu and is fluent in Xhosa, as well as being able to manage in several other dialects. In 1938 he joined the Assemblies of God in South Africa and began to preach with much blessing. He had a dream in which he heard the words, 'Africa must get back to God.' Out of this was born his 'Back to God Crusade' which took him all over South Africa conducting large tent meetings. For almost forty years the Crusade has worked its way systematically across South Africa. He has called into being about a thousand congregations. Multitudes have been won for Christ, and many of his young converts have entered the ministry. His first big Crusade was in 1945 in Port Elizabeth – there were a thousand converts in six weeks. But it was in East London (S. Africa) that the most remarkable work was done. The migration of the Bantus from their kraals into urban areas led to the break up of their tribal ties and society, resulting very often in crime, drunkenness and immorality. Bhengu declared war on sin and crime. Thousands were converted including thieves who returned stolen goods by the van load, and murderers who confessed and gave themselves up to justice. Many 'tsotsis' (African gangsters) were converted and some became able ministers of the gospel; but some of these hooligans were so incensed that they sought to kill him. Failing in that, some laid information with the police accusing Bhengu of being a receiver of stolen goods. He was soon cleared and the police realised what an amazing work was going on. Not only were stolen goods being returned by converted thieves, but hooligans were yielding up their flick knives and guns and weapons of all kinds. An amazed Major of Police told an Assemblies of God missionary from England (James E. Mullan), 'Mr. Mullan, we have confidence in Mr. Bhengu and we want this work to go on by all means.'

During those remarkable days in East London, God so poured out His Spirit that it was like the Acts of the Apostles all over again. As he preached the sick were healed. A cripple suddenly jumped up, shouted and threw away his crutches, he walked, then ran and there was an uproar. It was God at work! Nicholas Bhengu said, 'We didn't pray for him. Jesus healed him; and he shouted and the people knew that Jesus heals today.'

On another day a crowd of over 7,000 were assembled in the open air. While they were singing a simple Christian chorus the Holy Spirit fell upon them, just as He did upon the household of Cornelius when Peter was preaching in Acts 10. That was at half past ten in the morning, and that great crowd were still there when darkness fell. Small boys of just twelve years talked in tongues and prophesied. It was impossible for Bhengu or anyone else to preach. As on the Day of Pentecost, 'it was noised abroad' and people gathered from all over to see what the noise was. When they came into the revival atmosphere these sightseers too were converted. The numbers continued to increase and the Lord continued to save and baptise them with the Holy Ghost and fire.

The people were so under the power of God that they could not walk, many of them were prostrated and lay as though they were dead. Bhengu sent for buses to come and take the people to their homes, but as soon as the bus drivers and conductors tried to pick them up they themselves came under the power of the Holy Spirit. They said to Bhengu, 'As soon as we touch them this comes into us.' Very many of these bus drivers and conductors were converted. The result of the revival was such that a local theatre, a very big one, which had been very popular, had to close down because no one wanted to go any more. The owners begged Nicholas Bhengu and his followers to rent it from them.

Through the passing years the work has snowballed. Each year seems to witness fresh revivals. All classes of people have been reached. A Zulu Queen was baptised in 1971 in front of a crowd of 5,000 witnesses. Influential African political leaders are among the converts.

Now seventy five years of age, Bhengu is widely respected by both black, white and coloured throughout South Africa. He has preached throughout Africa, and has visited Japan, and ministered with great acceptance in Britain, Canada and America. He is also accepted by other denominations. For years he never rested, never took a holiday, he was consumed by the Divine Commission. Edwin Orr knows him and visited Bhengu in his East London Assembly. He says, 'It was a dynamic service. Shortly before my visit Bhengu had baptised thirteen hundred converts upon profession of faith before 7,000 witnesses at Eastertime.'

The story of Reinhard Bonnke is probably even more amazing than that of Bhengu. Reinhard Bonnke was born in 1940, the son of a German Pentecostal pastor. At the age of nine years he had his first call from God when the Lord told him that he would one day preach the

Gospel in Africa. At ten, he recalls, 'God called me, not directly, but through a preacher who delivered a message which deeply touched me.' When he told people that he was going to be a preacher and that God had called him to be a missionary in Africa, they just laughed. The smiles vanished, however, when a woman from a neighbouring village stood up in a prayer meeting and shared a vision the Lord had given her. She said, 'I saw a huge crowd of black people. In the middle of that crowd I saw a little boy holding a big loaf of bread and giving it to the black people.' Then she pointed at young Reinhard and declared, 'And that's the boy I've seen in the vision.'

When Bonnke was seventeen years old he had a vision in which he clearly saw a map of Africa. He explains, 'I saw one dot in the south and next to it was written Johannesburg. Now my geography was very weak. I had always thought that Johannesburg was much higher up, and so I got out a map. I looked and I saw that Johannesburg was there on the map where Johannesburg was in the vision. That convinced me of the genuineness of the vision.'

He trained at the Bible College of Wales in Swansea, which was founded by Rees Howells, who as well as being a great intercessor was also a great man of faith. That principle of 'living by faith' was instilled in the students and Bonnke acknowledges his debt to that great College. He learned to trust God in a practical way. In due time the missionary board of the church in Germany wanted to send him to Zambia. He had to tell them. 'Under no circumstances.' But when he explained to the board about his vision they readily agreed to send him to South Africa in 1967. For five years he worked in Lesotho.

The turning point in his ministry came at the beginning of a large crusade which he had organised in a large South African town, with an international evangelist with a special ministry of healing. The meetings were widely

advertised and the hall was full for the opening service.
Next morning, however, Bonnke met the evangelist and
found him with his bags packed ready to leave. Unable to
stop him going, Bonnke found himself faced with a very
difficult situation. He prayed and confessed, 'Lord, I am
not Mr. —, but I am your servant, and now I am going to
pray and preach and I will pray for the sick and you will
do the miracles.' Facing the crowd he had to tell them,
'That great man has gone, but Jesus is here.' As he
preached, the power of God fell upon that meeting and as
he ministered, God worked. He did not lay hands upon
the sick, but he felt the Holy Spirit was telling him to
pray for the blind. He asked, 'How many blind people
are here?' Some six people stood up in response. He told
them, 'I am not going to touch you, but Jesus will touch
you there where you are. I am going to rebuke that
blindness in the name of Jesus, and you are going to see
right now.' He commanded, 'In the Name of Jesus Christ
of Nazareth, blind eyes open!' Suddenly there were cries
of 'I can see. I can see!' One woman came to the platform
and said, 'for many years I was completely blind. Give
me something to read. I want to prove to you that I can
see.' She took the Bible and she read, her hands trembling with excitement. The great congregation erupted in
shouts of praise and thanksgiving to God. That was the
turning point in Reinhard Bonnke's ministry in Africa.

He founded a multi-racial team in liaison with Christ
For All Nations. One of his closest African associates
who has developed a great ministry of praying for the
sick and casting out demons is Michael Kolisang. Before
very long he was using a very large tent seating ten
thousand for his crusades. Over the period of the 1970s
and early 1980s he moved through Africa with growing
power. After a crusade in Batho in 1979, the Bloemfontein newspaper, *The Friend* ran this headline on the front
page: 'Surprise for Cops at Batho. Thieves return stolen
goods.' The story read, 'Hundred of Bloemfontein

thieves have seen the light. They have taken stolen goods back to the Batho Police Station in the Bloemfontein Township to be returned to their owners. The police at Batho have received three large truckloads of stolen goods, including blankets, tea-sets, mats and many other household necessities. The repentance followed a big crusade held near the Ikaelelo School at Kogisanong township recently. The evangelists of the crusade, Pastor Reinhard Bonnke, Michael Kolisang and Adam Mtsweni pleaded with the thousands of people who attended the healing mission to repent and follow the ways of true Christians.'

'Captain P. T. Rantsoareng of the Batho Criminal Investigation Department has asked anyone who has lost household goods to come forward and identify them at the Batho Police Station.'

Up to between 10,000 and 15,000 people attended a single service in that crusade, with many hundreds of conversions – including twenty policemen!

In 1980, Bonnke preached at the Assemblies of God Conference at Minehead, Somerset, England. Over 7,000 people were present in the holiday camp which was taken over for the week. It was the writer's privilege to have close fellowship with him, his wife, and his African colleague Michael Kolisang throughout that memorable week. The final meeting on the Friday evening was one that none of those present will ever forget. Seasoned Pentecostals all recognised that the hand of God was upon his humble servant. His preaching of the Gospel was attended with unusual power throughout the whole week. In September, 1981 he returned to Britain for a two-week Crusade in Birmingham Town Hall, organised by the United Pentecostal Churches in the area. On the last day, people began queuing up at 2.30 p.m. for the evening meeting and about four hundred people had to be turned away as the hall was full. There were some seven hundred decisions for Christ registered during the two weeks and some outstanding healings, including that of an eighty-six year old lady from Coventry who shouted with joy, 'I can walk, I can walk!' It was the first time in ten years that she had been able to get around without the aid of sticks or crutches. The case of a local charity worker from Tipton who gave himself up to the police after the crusade, made the headlines on the front page of the Birmingham Evening Mail, after he had appeared in Dudley Magistrates Court. He confessed to stealing from Dudley Council for Voluntary Services when he had run short of cash. He told the police, 'It came over me that I'd done wrong and I want to give the money back. If it wasn't for the preacher I might have continued to do wrong. But his sermon shook me out of that, I cried when I listened to his words.'

Throughout 1982–3 Bonnke continued to preach with increasing power throughout Africa and in many parts of the world, including New Zealand, Germany, and Korea, and most notably in Finland, where hundreds responded to the altar calls in the huge Ice Stadium in Helsinki, and many miracles of healing took place. Crowds of ten thousand nightly flocked to hear him and he was headline news in the national press and on television. One of Helsinki's main newspapers, *Iltalehti* carried the Bonnke crusade as its main news item on the front page. It was headlined, 'Signs and Wonders Today.' The reporter noted that 'when the hall emptied there were many pairs of crutches left leaning against the platform.'

Reinhard Bonnke's great burden, however, is for Africa. That is where he believes God has called him to labour. Throughout Southern Africa his 10,000-seater tent has been too small in recent days to contain the crowds. In 1980 some 100,000 people made decisions for Christ in his crusades; and that figure has probably been surpassed in each succeeding year. He has gone to the most difficult places such as Soweto and met with equally great results. Everywhere thieves have made restitution to prove the genuineness of their repentance; witchdoctors have renounced their profession and destroyed their idols and paraphernalia; drug addicts have been delivered; and believers have been filled with the Holy Spirit and have spoken in tongues. In areas where he has been it is claimed on good authority that the crime rate has dropped by over thirty per cent.

In 1979 he started to plan for a bigger tent. The final concept was staggering, the world's biggest tent to seat over 30,000 people. It cost well over a million pounds, with many extras for great trucks to transport this tent around Africa. His vision is to take the gospel from Cape Town to Cairo. In 1983 he preached in Zaire, Zimbabwe, and Uganda with the same response and with requests and plans for him to return with his 30,000-seater tent. The making of the tent has been quite a test of faith; many difficulties were encountered as nothing of this magnitude had ever been constructed before. It is so big that not even the new Ellis Park stadium in Johannesburg could accommodate it: the ground area is too small. The Durban-based *Sunday Tribune* in a banner headline called it 'Seventh-Storey Heaven.' The tent is the equivalent of a seven-storey building in height.

The new tent was used for the first time at the end of 1983 when it was erected at KwaThema. In the two weeks crusade, eight thousand said 'Yes' to Jesus. A reporter, Betty Lore, who was in the new tent said, 'I stood with wordless amazement as I gazed upward at the roof of the tent tabernacle, seven-storeys high. The interior size of the new tent is breathtaking. Laid out in seemingly endless rows were the benches. A few came from afar to ponder this engineering wonder. However, the majority who came under the majestic ceiling of the tent seemed oblivious of the tremendous engineering and logistic feat that has been achieved. The crowds came intent only on experiencing what God was doing inside. With hungry hearts and many sick bodies thousands came, despite the icy cold. And they were not disappointed. Hundreds were instantly healed, but more thrilling than these wonderful testimonies was the count of nearly 8,000 who registered a decision to make Jesus their personal Saviour.'

The tent was officially opened on the 18th February, 1984. It was erected close to Soweto and the dedication of the tent for the service of the Lord in evangelism in Africa was attended by people from all over Africa and a large contingent from overseas as well. Reinhard Bonnke believes that Africa is on the verge of the greatest revival in its history, and he sees the tent as a great combine harvester, which will roll from Cape Town to Cairo. He and his team believe that God will triple their harvest of souls to 300,000 per year in the 'Big Tent'. Prayer, frequently with fasting, is one of the secrets of the power of God resting upon Reinhard Bonnke and his team.

Such is the move of God's Spirit in Africa that the world's largest tent has proved too small to contain the crowds flocking to hear the gospel. In the Spring of 1990 Reinhard Bonnke gave away his great tent to a group working in Mozambique. He is now attracting crowds numbered in the hundreds of thousands. Equipped with high powered amplifying equipment he is geared to be able to address crowds of up to one million. The response to the gospel is increasing all the time. The wind of God's revival power is blowing across Africa.

13

Indonesia – Revolution and Revival

Indonesia, one-time hotbed of Communism has since 1965 been dominated by an entirely different kind of revolution. Although conflicting reports have circulated throughout the religious press, there is no doubt that the Holy Spirit has been (and still is) mightily at work in these islands. 'Not in 1,300 years has there ever been such a breakthrough,' states the Rev. Gering, a resident missionary. 'Moslems are coming to Christ by the tens of thousands. In the past only about one half of those converted to Christianity were ever baptised because they were murdered by their families before they could take this step. But this is all different now.'

When one realises that Indonesia consists of over 13,000 islands (about 3,000 of which are inhabited), covering some 735,900 square miles, with a population of 150 million, then it is understandable that there will inevitably be widely differing reports from different parts and all under the 'umbrella' of Indonesia. Java is the largest with a population of 81 million. There are over two hundred languages and dialects, but Bahasa Indonesia is the national language.

A brief statement of the historical background is essential to the full appreciation of the present movement of

130

God. Between the fifth and fifteenth centuries was the Hindu and Buddhist period; Islam entered in the thirteenth century and grew in influence to the sixteenth century, when the Portuguese brought Indonesia under European influence. It was under Dutch colonial rule for some three hundred years, until they finally relinquished control in 1949, after Indonesia had claimed her independence in 1945.

The story of the Indonesian revival is an illustration of God's sovereignty. The 1st October, 1965 was the date fixed by the Indonesian Communist Party (the largest outside of Russia and China) to stage a complete national take-over. Their strategy required the deaths of eight leading generals in order to eliminate organised military resistance. This plan would have succeeded had it not been for two of the generals escaping and leading a triumphant counter-attack.

One of the prominent figures on the political scene was a Christian, Darius Marpaung, who headed the Indonesian Christian Workers Union at that time. In the upheaval he emerged to lead the 'Communist Opposition' groups in their strategy of publicly exposing the true nature of Communism. These tactics reached their climax at a mass rally in Jakarta. Tens of thousands filled the capital to hear Darius Marpaung deliver a dynamic speech challenging the government to 'purge the Communists from the Cabinet.' Marpaung later confessed his sense of destiny as he stood at the rostrum, and his deep dependence upon God to enable him to make that key speech. President Sukarno had no alternative but to surrender to the anti-communist pressures from the people and the military.

Don Crawford, reporter and author of the book *Miracles in Indonesia* interviewed a former Indonesian member of parliament who bluntly declared, 'The Communist defeat was a miracle of God . . . after all they were just two heartbeats away from victory.' Lists were

131

discovered later of those whom the Communists proposed to eliminate, once they had gained power. In addition to political opponents the lists included religious leaders and the expulsion of all foreign missionaries. God intervened at a crucial moment in Indonesia's history!

Suharto, one of the successful generals, was appointed president in place of Sukarno. He undoubtedly saved the country from economic collapse, but it was under his presidency that one of the most savage and bloody purges ever known in this area took place. The anti-communist blood-letting did not abate until some 400,000 people had been butchered.

The Communists in their reach for power had aroused the bitter opposition of the Muslim population and the subsequent massacres were carried out with the blessing of the Muslim leaders. However, the fanatical savagery that saw thousands of Communists executed without trial, had a back-lash effect upon many of the young Muslim students. They were so sickened by it that they rejected their own faith.

These ex-Muslim students saw for themselves the stark contrast in the behaviour of the small groups of Christians. Far from indulging in bloodshed, they saw the Christians expressing Christ's own command, 'Love your enemies, bless them that curse you, do good to them that hate you.' The Christians buried abandoned bodies, they sheltered widows and orphans, and sometimes at risk to their own lives, they sheltered known Communists. This convincing demonstration of real Christianity was undoubtedly a key factor in the ensuing revival.

Communism was a comparatively modern influence, but animism and the occult had bound and dominated the islands for centuries. Many islands were notorious centres for all forms of black magic and demonic religions. The Dutch missionaries who first preached the Gospel in this region had made little impact because of this evil dominance. Only a supernatural gospel could break through the centuries of darkness and fear. The Pentecostals met with more success and today, the aftermath of the revival of 1965 finds them by far the strongest group. One of the early Pentecostal missionaries was Cornelius Groesbeek who arrived in what was then the Dutch East Indies in January 1921, from Bethel Temple of Seattle, Washington, U.S.A. Soon after his arrival he was summoned to the palace of a Balinese king to pray for the king's daughter who was very ill. The Rev. Groesbeek prayed for the girl and she was miraculously healed. The king then revealed to the missionary that he had had a dream in which he had seen a man and had been told to call for the man to pray for his daughter. 'You are the man I saw in my dreams,' he said. The Rev. Groesbeek then told the king, 'And you, your majesty, are the man I saw in a vision when the Lord' called me to your island.' This was typical of the many miracles that accompanied the early message of Pentecost in Indonesia, says the Rev. A. H. Mandey, General Secretary of Geredja Pantecosta di Indonesia. The work grew steadily, but the outbreak of World War II and then the Japanese occupation during the years 1942–45 stopped all missionary work. However, during this period, rather than closing churches, the Pentecostal Church in Indonesia grew under their own capable leadership.

The 1940s closed with a struggle for independence amid hard times, but the church met the test and stood victorious through war and poverty. After the war missionary work was resumed and there were fresh influxes of missionaries from New Zealand and Australia.

After the abortive coup in 1965, to combat Communism there was a government decree insisting that every Indonesian have some kind of religion. This was no doubt a factor also in the awakening. Before the revival there was very little response by Muslims to the gospel. In two of the most fanatical Muslim areas – Atjeh in the far north and Seravai in the south, conversions were counted in ones and twos. The few Christians in these areas had moved in from other islands. W.E.C. missionaries entered South Sumatra in 1953 and established a ministry among the migrants but were unable to penetrate the Muslim resistance. Then just before Independence, a young Muslim leader of the Seravai tribe was converted. His conversion opened up that community to the gospel. A team from the Indonesian Bible Institute, led by one of their well-known evangelists called Octavianus, visited them and a good number of key people in the Seravai tribe were converted. A church was formed which grew to 300 members within months. Immediately they faced Islamic persecution. Converted Muslims were threatened with death, torture and beatings. Some succumbed, but by 1965 the number was again up to three hundred. A second team of evangelists from Batu visited the area. The numbers tripled, and a Bible School was established to train leaders.

Then came the Communist take-over bid. In the savage anti-Communist reaction that followed, fanatical Muslims were given a chance to attack the Christians as well. The fact that many Christians had offered refuge to distraught Communists left them vulnerable. God's sovereign care was revealed, however. The Police Inspector who had just been appointed to the area was a Christian. To protect believers from fanatical Muslims, he ordered those who were in danger to be placed in prison as 'Communist sympathisers' for their own protection. Christians found themselves in prison alongside actual Communists. The Christians encouraged one another and boldly shared their faith with the Communists, with the result that many Communists were converted. What had begun as a plot to destroy Christianity only served to spread it. When the prison doors opened after things had cooled down, the number of Christians had already multiplied.

The island of Timor has been especially blessed since 1965 when a Javanese evangelistic team visited it. The team consisted mainly of students from the Batu Bible School, and their message directed the listeners to a simple but complete trust in God. The response in the Soe area of the island was staggering. Church leaders at last made a complete break with the occult, burning amulets to testify to their new commitment. When people saw that they came to no harm from evil spirits they were encouraged to follow their example. This experience of a living faith swept away the customs of palm wine intoxication and seeking the narcotic influence derived from chewing the betel nut. Prayer meetings increased and new evangelistic teams sprang up from the ranks of the young people, who before 1965 had been the hardest and most unresponsive of the Indonesian population. The gospel of deliverance began to kindle throughout the nation. It was evangelism 'with signs following' in the New Testament order of demons being cast out and the sick healed.

Marion Allen of the Christian and Missionary Alliance closely investigated the happenings in the Soe area. He stated that almost every type of New Testament miracle had been witnessed. The miraculous confirmation of the gospel has been a major factor in the phenomenal growth of the church in Timor. In the first three years of this revival some 200,000 converts were added to the churches. As to the quality and effectiveness of these converts, it is significant that prayer is the first priority with these Indonesian believers. Seven days a week believers meet between 4 a.m. and 5 a.m. One pastor heard of high school students meetings for early morning prayer and checked up on them. He found that after prayer they had a list of sick people in their immediate area who needed prayer. They went out and prayed for every sick person and they saw every one of them healed.

The head of a theological school was sent on a tour of

investigation. In one major city he asked if the revival had had any effect on crime. They replied, 'Look at the jail, the door is open and there is nobody in there.' The area was notorious for cattle thieving but nobody was stealing cows any more.

Frank L. Cooley, an American Presbyterian missionary, conducted a broad analytical study of Indonesian Christianity in the late 1970s. He said, 'I see the Holy Spirit very active on a wide variety of fronts, in some places where we don't even look for it. I think the Church in Indonesia is going to keep right on growing. The rapid growth has forced churches to examine their statements of faith and subject their ecclesiastical position to Biblical analysis, and some inherited positions have been altered with Biblical insight. This is evidence to me of the depth of the Holy Spirit's work here.'

In Janury 1984 the writer was privileged to interview New Zealand missionary, Harvey John Walker on his arrival in England from the Tawangmango Bible School, Indonesia, where he had been on the staff since 1975. His parents first went as missionaries to Indonesia in 1949, when Harvey was five years old. They commenced working on the island of Timor, and then moved to the island of Rote. They later moved to Java where they established a Bible School in Malang. Their next move was to Jakarta and then to Bali, where they were in 1965 at the time of the abortive Communist uprising. (Harvey left for schooling in 1960, and returned in 1975 but was constantly in touch with the situation in Indonesia through his family.) Speaking of the revival, Harvey Walker says, 'I think the greatest thing that I have heard and that I have seen in the revival is people being convicted of sin and of their need for the Saviour. During the last ten years the revival has gathered momentum. There have been healings and all sorts of things happening all over Indonesia, but in general terms it has been people repenting and coming to God.'

'My father's great vision was for Bible School work and that is still a great need today. In our Bible School in Tawanmango we have some 130 to 140 students in each year for the two year course. The students come from all denominations and from all over Indonesia. Many of them go out and establish churches. It is extremely exciting and rewarding work.'

In 1973 there were about 8 million Protestants in Indonesia, according to Rev. A. H. Mandey. Harvey Walker says that there has been church growth of around 200 per cent in the last fifteen years, and there are now approaching 14 million Protestants, of whom around 11 million or more are Pentecostals. These are divided into some eighty different groups, the largest of which has some 5,000 churches with about 3 million members, this being the Pentecostal Church of Indonesia, which stemmed from America. The revival in Indonesia has now matured; it has probably lost the flamboyance which characterised its early stages but it is certainly not finished. It is still going on and, according to Harvey Walker, Christian leaders in Indonesia are saying that ten thousand pastors would be swallowed up over night if they were available. That's revival!

14

The Korean Pentecost

Billy Graham says, 'The Korean church has set a pattern of perennial revival to which the Church universal looks with wonder and amazement.' Yet, until the second half of the last century, Korea remained shut to the gospel. In 1866, Robert Thomas, a Welshman serving in China as a missionary, went to Korea to distribute Bibles amongst the Chinese speaking people there. On arrival his ship was given a hostile reception by the 'half-savage' Korean coastguards. As it came close to land they attacked it and threw burning brands on the deck. The crew were forced to abandon the burning vessel. Some managed to get into the small boat but they were captured and killed. Brave Robert Thomas gathered some of his Bibles and began to wade through the shallow water to land. On the shore he was savagely attacked, but he pressed his precious Bibles into the hands of his murderers before he collapsed and died. 'And so the soil of North Korea drank the blood of a martyr on the very same spot where forty years later, the revival took place . . .' says René Monod in his fascinating book, *The Korean Revival*.

In 1876 the Japanese navy forced an entry into several Korean ports; other naval powers followed them, until in 1884, primitive, isolated Korea at last officially opened her gates to the world – and the gospel with the arrival of American missionary Dr. Allen. In 1885 more missionaries arrived; the Appensellers (Methodists) and the Underwoods (Presbyterian). There was steady growth from the first and some stirrings of the Spirit as when Pastor R. A. Hardie of America preached there in 1903. 'The fire of the Holy Spirit that rose up in Hardie's meeting, spread throughout the entire land. That was the beginning of the Pentecostal movement in Korea,' says Yonggi Cho. But it was in 1907 that God gave something very special to the infant Korean church. Korea 1907 is a date to match Wales 1904 and America 1857.

Most of the missionaries at that time were American, and when America sanctioned the Japanese occupation of Korea – for 2,000 years Japan and China had vied for the country – the missionaries found themselves placed in a tense situation. They started special prayer meetings. Half of the missionaries were conservative Presbyterians and faithful to the Word of God. News of the 1904 Welsh Revival had quickly reached Welsh Presbyterian missionaries labouring in India in the hills of Assam. As they prayed with renewed faith for a similar visitation, revival broke out amongst them with results as striking as those 'back home in the Welsh valleys.' News of this awakening in Assam reached their Presbyterian colleagues in Korea, who were likewise moved to pray for revival. Dr. Edwin Orr says, 'In August, 1906, these missionaries at Pyongyang met for a week of prayer and Bible study. They had a deep concern for the need of the country in its time of humiliation. They studied the First Epistle of John, which afterwards became their textbook in revival work. The winter months saw them absorbed in preparing intensive Bible study for the Korean Church. It was customary for representatives of area churches to come from far and wide at the New Year for Bible study. In spite of opposition, a strange new spirit entered the meeting of fifteen hundred men. So many of them wanted to pray that the leader told the whole audience, 'If you want to pray like that, all pray.' A faithful American missionary, Dr. Lee, was the leader and he described what followed, 'A tide began to sweep through the church. There was no confusion; it was a single harmony of prayer, as if voices of all the praying congregation merged together to form a single cry to God. The Holy Ghost welded them all together into one. At this great prayer meeting one worshipper after another rose, confessed his sins, and then fell to his knees again, weeping and begging God for forgiveness.' The meetings carried on day after day, with confessions of sins, weeping and trembling. The heathen were astounded. The delegates to the New Year gathering carried the revival to their various churches. Always the results were the same: deep conviction of sin, followed by confession and restitution, plus the new feature of audible prayer in unison – a feature which continues to this day in some churches in Korea.

René Monod says, 'Deadly enemies made their peace with one another; stolen money and goods were returned. Past injustices were set right, not only between Christians, but to pagans as well. One old Chinese businessman was much surprised when a Christian returned a large sum of money which he had once received from the merchant in error. Many heathens were converted and brought to Christ by the honourable conduct of these Christians.'

Without this tremendous work of the Holy Spirit it is doubtful whether the church in Korea could have survived the long bitter years of unceasing conflict with the government and with the powers of darkness. The long years of Japanese occupation brought problems to the Christians. Once a year the Japanese required all Koreans to show their loyalty to the government by attending a ceremony at the Shinto shrine. This came to a head during the 1930s when the Japanese were trying to assimilate the Koreans and trying to inculcate loyalty to the Emperor. Christians struggled with their consciences. 'Was it right for them to bow down before a Shinto shrine?' The Japanese 'explained' that the rite was political not religious, but Christians were unhappy as all the prayers were Shintoist in nature. Finally one brave Korean pastor ventured to absent himself from the ceremony. The Japanese reaction was swift and ruthless: he was beaten to death near the Shinto shrine. Many Christians were encouraged by his faith, but others found the price too much and at this time the revival began to decline.

The end of World War II in 1945 at last released Korea from Japanese occupation, but more terrible times of suffering loomed ahead. During the brief period of peace, the Christians – especially in North Korea – concentrated on building up the work of God and erecting churches. As Dr. K. S. Latourette reminds us in his monumental work, *Expansion of Christianity*, 'After World War II, Korea tried to form an independent government. But Russia and the United States had set up zones of occupation divided by the 38th parallel of latitude. North of that parallel the Russians stimulated the formation of the North Korean People's Government, a Communist regime. In the South, with the encouragement and aid of the U.S., the Republic of Korea came into being and in 1948 was recognised by the United Nations as the sole legitimate government of Korea.' Syngman Rhee, a born again Methodist, was the first President.

The Christians in North Korea were soon subjected to the most cruel persecutions by the Communists. Thousands fled to the freedom of South Korea, but as long as freedom remained, believers gathered daily for great prayer meetings. The Communists reacted by closing church after church, but nothing could stop the prayer surge. Prayer meetings grew to even greater proportions than those of 1906–7. These prayer meetings were held at sunrise – around 5 a.m. In all kinds of weather, thousands gathered, and all prayed simultaneously as in the early days of the revival. At times 10,000 men and women were in a prayer meeting, praying in a unison only possible by the over-ruling co-ordination of the Spirit of God.

This roused the wrath of the Communists and they responded with the most fiendish tortures. The blood of martyrs flowed again. Several Christians were crucified by the Chinese Communists. Faithful witnesses who still preached the gospel had their tongues cut out by the Reds. Children caught at a secret Sunday School were deafened by having chopsticks rammed into their ear-drums.

'In June 1950, equipped with Russian arms, tanks and planes, the North Koreans surged across the 38th parallel and quickly overran most of the South. Under American initiative, the Security Council of the United Nations sent forces to Korea, chiefly American, and drove back the North Koreans. Chinese Communist 'volunteer' armies came to the rescue. The battle line swayed back and forth. After months of fighting, in July 1953, an armistice was signed which was in effect an uneasy truce.' (K. S. Latourette).

In fact, that 'Peace Conference' at Panmunjom still grinds on to the present time. However, the influx of thousands of Christians from the North served to strengthen the church in South Korea. Revival broke out in Seoul as the bloody war was coming to an end.

The Methodists and Presbyterians experienced great blessing; souls came to Christ and hundreds of new churches were built. Bob Pierce and Billy Graham visited war-torn Korea and experienced the power of true revival. Billy Graham said, 'When I visited Korea years ago I was astonished to find Christians getting up two hours before daylight, and gathering in their churches for prayer, Bible reading and testimony. The scenes I witnessed there have stayed with me through the years, and have had a great impact on my personal, spiritual life.'

Dr. Robert V. Finley, missionary and founder of International Students Inc., was in Korea in the early 1950s. He also confessed to being deeply moved, 'In Korea, this Baptist had his theological stronghold shaken to its very foundations! I was in a prayer meeting in Korea when fifty people, whom we would call incurable, were instantaneously, miraculously healed! Until then I had it all figured out dispensationally that things like this did not happen any more. But what are you going to do when you see them take place right before your eyes? I figured there was just one thing for me to do, that was change my theology! Don't worry, I am still a good Baptist, but I learned that the New Testament is being fulfilled today just as much as in the first century. Any miracle you read about in the book of Acts has been duplicated among "the young churches of Asia" including the raising of the dead! I have seen it happen – not just once, but more than once.'

For such staggering claims, a second witness is called for, and readily found in the form of René Monod, who witnessed similar happenings in Korean Presbyterian churches, 'I had always been of the opinion that miracles were reserved for the early Christians. A lame man was brought to the meeting; several Koreans had taken turns to carry him 80 kilometres on their backs. Now the cripple lay there before the congregation. His weak leg and arm were shorter than the sound limbs. Prayers were said for him, and blood and the power of movement came back into the wasted limbs. The lame man stretched, stood up and tried out his healed limbs. They were no longer short; the sick, wasted leg and arm had grown to the normal length of the sound ones. I would never have believed reports of this miracle if I had not seen it for myself. The church where that happened had had a turnout of two thousand members at the 5 a.m. prayer meeting every morning for five years. In the face of such faith and devotion, can we still wonder that all the miracles of the New Testament were manifested again in the Korean revival? I admit that I had always doubted whether the dead could be raised in the twentieth century. Since my first visit to Korea, which was followed by others, I have doubted no longer.'

In 1954 a staunch young Buddhist lay dying of tuberculosis, having been given only some three months to live by the doctors. Through the visits and faithful witness of a young Christian girl he eventually surrendered his life to Christ. The tears of this eighteen year old girl deeply moved him as she pleaded with him to receive Christ. She left him with her Bible which he read and not only was he gloriously converted but within a short time he was healed. Within a few years he completed Bible School training and began to pastor a tent church in a slum area of Seoul. Today his name is known around the world as the pastor of the largest church in the world, his name is Paul Yonggi Cho.

The tent was just an old American marine tent – and it leaked badly when it rained. Yonggi Cho says, 'Those were days of struggle. When it rained, we had to place buckets in strategic places to catch the leaks that would trickle through the handsewn tent roof. My congregation was poor, and their lives were empty of everything except problems. The days in the tent church were often days of discouragement. There were several times I packed my bags and was ready to get on a train and leave.' But he stuck it out and God taught him the great principles of faith which have made him one of the most significant Christian leaders in the world today.

In that humble tent people with all kinds of diseases and problems were healed and helped. Gradually the congregation began to increase and they moved downtown to the West Gate area of Seoul. They then had some six hundred members. In 1972 Billy Graham was the first to preach in the magnificent new building in Yoido, the government district of Seoul. The Full Gospel Central Church when first erected was capable of seating 10,000. Since then it has been further enlarged to accommodate the ever-increasing membership. On 31 May, 1981 it had 177,489 adult members, all active participants in the 12,421 home cells. Before the end of 1981 the membership reached 200,000

Dr. Yonggi Cho was the guest preacher at the British Assemblies of God Conference at Minehead in May 1981. It was the writer's privilege to share close fellowship during that week with Dr. Cho and it was humbling to be in the prsence of such a remarkable and totally unspoilt servant of God. He remains unaffected by his tremendous success, and unmoved by the publicity he receives. One is left in no doubt as to the secret of the success of the ever-growing church in Seoul – it is prayer, and prayer with fasting. His faith staggers one. At that conference he declared that he was believing God that the congregation would have reached 500,000 by 1984. The writer frankly was staggered in unbelief and thought that, for once, dear Dr. Cho had gone too far.

However, in 1987 it was my privilege to visit Korea and test the reality of all this for myself. I felt like the Queen of Sheba after she had visited Solomon – dumbfounded, and with her could only exclaim that the half had not been told me. For once I found that the truth surpassed the stories and claims. The membership had then passed the half million mark and was 537,000.

A most careful check is kept on the membership. An ultra-modern computer ensures that the figures are accurate and up to date. By January 1990 the membership was well in excess of 700,000. The next target is 1 million and it is well within their sights.

In 1973 they established what is called their prayer mountain. Situated some 45 km north of Seoul, it is strategically placed between the capital of South Korea and the border with North Korea.

The person behind this great concept is a remarkable woman of prayer, Dr Jashil Choi, Yonggi Cho's mother-in-law. It was the thrill of a lifetime to talk to her and participate in the great gatherings on Prayer Mountain with her. Every day of the year people can be found praying, and many fasting as well. One can always depend on three thousand people being present, and at weekends the number swells to at least ten thousand, while on special occasions they are able to cope with crowds of twenty-five thousand. In 1986 they erected a massive hall capable of holding ten thousand. In addition there are several other buildings as well as accommodation blocks providing overnight accommodation for three thousand and more. They go with one great purpose in mind: PRAYER, and prayer for revival is always high on the agenda. That is one of the Korean church's open secrets – prayer, prayer and more prayer.

Although Dr Cho and his church are the best known and certainly the largest church in Korea, yet they are only a part of what God is doing in this remarkable nation. The largest Methodist church, the largest Presbyterian church, the largest Baptist church, and the largest Pentecostal church, are all to be found in Seoul. Each of them majors on prayer, with regular periods of fasting. All of them have multi services to cope with the numbers, and all of them are aggressively evangelistic and committed to world missions. There is an atmosphere of continuous revival throughout South Korea.

The great majority of churches throughout Korea have regular all-nights of prayer. There are some one hundred prayer mountains throughout the nation and these are centres of concentrated prayer and seeking God. In the 1984 centennial of the introduction of protestant missions in Korea, over one million gathered on the great boulevard which was once an air-strip for war planes in the Korean War.

Korean Christians exploited the opportunity presented

to them in 1987 when Seoul hosted the Olympic Games. They gave themselves to intense prayer for many months beforehand, and when the visitors poured in from scores of nations they were ready to witness to them and present them with Christian gospel literature in their own language. Only eternity will reveal what was accomplished and how many nations have been influenced by the witness of the new converts who were won for Christ during the Korean Olympic Games.

The burden of Korean Christians is to make their nation a truly Christian nation. Well over 25 per cent are Christians and the numbers are growing daily. They also have a special burden for North Korea and the day may not be far distant when North Korea will follow in the steps of the communist countries in Eastern Europe and throw off the oppressive yoke of communism. The day that happens will be a wonderful one in the history of this unique nation. Revival could sweep through North Korea and the united Korean nation could well spread revival throughout Asia, Japan, and could even swing the battle in China.

15

The China Miracle

China, the largest nation containing one fifth of the world's population, is almost certainly the scene for the greatest revival of them all. China has witnessed several remarkable revivals in the last one hundred and twenty years. Revivals took place before, during and after Mao's cataclysmic rise to power which resulted in such severe persecution of Christians. Although information is still scanty and hard to come by, it is becoming increasingly clear that the Church has not only survived since the Communist take-over in 1949, but has thrived as never before. This giant nation of one thousand million people is witnessing a great awakening of a truly indigenous Chinese Church, the creation of the Holy Spirit.

In 1983, Dr. J. Hudson Taylor III, General Director of the Overseas Missionary Fellowship (OMF) and great grandson of Hudson Taylor, founder of the China Inland Mission, predecessor of the OMF, declared that Protestant missionary endeavour in China had not been a failure. Speaking at a missionary convention in Toronto he maintained that, 'Even though foreign missionaries have been barred from mainland China since 1951, recent reports indicate that missionary labours of the past provided a base from which a vibrant church has developed.'

Critics of missionary endeavours hastily suggested that the many years of effort in China had yielded few enduring results and that the Chinese church had quickly folded after the Communist takeover in 1949. Events are now proving that the often costly missionary efforts of this century have not been in vain. This century, which dawned in China to the terrible Boxer Rising, when over a hundred missionaries were murdered along with thousands of their Chinese converts, looks like closing with the greatest missionary harvest of all time. Again and again the blood of the martyrs has only proved to be the seed of the Church.

Edwin Orr records, 'The Christian and Missionary Alliance noted that 1908 was a year of glorious revival in South China. The revival was still going on in 1911. Into the year 1911 the revival seethed. Prayer meetings in Honan Province drew great crowds to pray together as a mighty wave of prayer seemed to sweep over the place. The revival in China in these years proved to be the beginning of an indigenous spirit in the Chinese churches. In spite of opposition, a way was being prepared for the coming of greater awakening among the Chinese Christians who had come of age at last.'

John Sung, a pastor's son, was the link between the revivals of the first decade and the third decade of this century in China. His father had broken down in tears as a new awareness of his own sinfulness came over him as he preached on the Good Friday morning in 1907. Conviction spread through the whole congregation in Hinghwa and soon (says Leslie Lyall in his biography of John Sung), 'everyone was on his face before God confessing his sin. Reconciliation and restitution followed.' The revived church began witnessing with a new power and in two months there were 3,000 converts: another Pentecost indeed. Many new churches were built in the area and the work lifted to a new plane of spirituality. But perhaps the most significant happening that Good Friday was to Pastor Sung's nine year old boy whose bitter tears soaked through the lapel of his coat as the preacher described Jesus in the Garden of Gethsemane. Young

John Sung's spiritual life lapsed as he grew up. He gained a scholarship to a college in America and majored in science, gaining the highest honours. He pursued advanced studies at Ohio University, gaining degrees as MSc. and PhD. He was then offered a scholarship at Union Theological Seminary in New York.

At 'Union', John Sung found the approach to the Christian faith extremely liberal. His faith was adversely affected but at a powerful evangelistic service at a Baptist Church his faith was renewed. It was on the 10th February, 1927, which happened to be a year of revival in China. 'So great was his joy of forgiveness and concern to witness that he forgot that it was midnight and wakened his classmates with his vocal praise,' says Edwin Orr. Alas, the college authorities decided he was 'unbalanced' and the College President had him put in a lunatic asylum for six months! There alone with his Bible, John Sung claimed that he learned more of true theology than all he had heard in the lecture halls. He read the Bible through forty times. Through the intervention of a friend he was released, and returned to China. At home, his parents were soon aware that his 'mental unbalance' was really spiritual balance. He immediately began preaching, attended with great power. The secret was his intense prayer life: people were won for Christ and churches revived.

In 1931, John Sung linked with the famous Andrew Gih of the Bethel Worldwide Evangelistic Band. The association lasted about two and a half years and was very fruitful. Orr states that 'Gih and the Bethel Bands he founded did more to extend the revival in China than any other agency.' John Sung died in the prime of life, after only fifteen years of active service, but his influence was tremendous. In the opinion of Edwin Orr he was one of China's greatest evangelists of all time. He was God's revival messenger to the Chinese Church of his generation. In a tribute a Chinese leader (Peter Chung) called him 'the apostle of revival.'

Another 'mighty man of God' was a Confucian scholar by the name of Hsi, who took the name of Sheng-mo, 'Conqueror of Demons.' He is generally referred to as Pastor Hsi. He had been an opium addict when he entered a literary competiton for the best essay in classical style on the subject of Jesus as portrayed in Mark's Gospel. The study of the Gospel led to his conversion and effected a radical transformation in his life, including deliverance from his opium addiction. He became an evangelist and moved like an apostle 'planting churches' in city after city. He set up a rescue mission to help drug addicts find deliverance. His own wife was delivered from demon possession in a striking way after Hsi had prayed and fasted. It was New Testament Christianity in the power and demonstration of the Spirit of God.

The various movings of the Holy Spirit were all a providential preparation for the coming persecution. On 1st October, 1949, Mao Tse-tung proclaimed the People's Republic of China with the words, 'Today the Chinese people stand erect.' By the time of his death in 1976, Chairman Mao had secured an unenviable place in the 'Guiness Book of World Records' as responsible for the deaths of more people than any other person who ever lived. When Mao came to power in 1949 it is estimated that a staggering 50 million people were liquidated by the Communists – many of them Christians. 'No-one will ever know how many Christians were martyred for their faith,' says P. J. Johnstone in *Operation World*. All missionaries were banished, all churches were disbanded and declared illegal as the Communists sought to remove all traces of Christianity.

Paul Kauffman, who was born in China of pioneer missionary parents and operates a literature programme from Hong Kong, maintains that, 'China is opening up like a flower.' He believes that God's sovereign over-ruling in Red China is preparing the way for a greater freedom which will open it to the gospel. He cites the way that the ruthless Communist regime has broken the hold of centuries in such things as the 'absolute parental control system,' which precluded any individual from deciding his own destiny. Whilst opposing Christianity, the Communists have virtually destroyed the hold of the centuries of heathenism. The language barrier which was in itself a great wall with over three hundred different dialects, has been bulldozed by the Communist insistence that there is now just one official language – Mandarin Chinese. Communication is now much easier. The same applies to the Communists simplifying what has been the world's most complex written language. What has happened in China under the Communists is as hard for us to understand as was God's revealing to Habakkuk that He was going to use the Chaldeans to effect His purposes (Habakkuk 1:5–6). Nevertheless, the outcome reveals that God has been doing an amazing work during the period in which China was closed to all missionaries.

At a meeting of the Executive Board of Church Growth International in Seoul, Korea in 1983, Mama Kwong revealed that revival, fanned by the fires of persecution, is sweeping China today. Yonggi Cho interpreted for her and a leading Australian pastor of Assemblies of God, Reginald Klimionok, reported Mama Kwong's amazing story in the Australian Evangel.

She was first imprisoned in April 1961 for conducting a major evangelistic campaign in which many people were healed and many came to know the Lord and volunteered to become preachers. Mama Kwong says that the thirty-five years of Communist rule in China can be divided into four periods.

During the first period (1949–58), the communists expelled all 6,000 missionaries. They demanded that the Church be independent and self-supporting. In this way they could sever all fellowship with the foreign Church. They closed most of the churches, first in the country, then in the cities. They kept a few churches open in the cities so that visiting foreigners would think that there was freedom of worship in China. Underground Christians were arrested and nobody under the age of eighteen years was allowed to attend church.

In the second period (1958–66) everything was nationalised. People were starving and there was fierce oppression from the government. There was no freedom. If anyone complained they were imprisoned. Anyone found with a Bible was also imprisoned.

Mama Kwong says that during those days, God chose three hundred dedicated Christians to start a new church. As they gathered at 3 a.m. one morning, they saw a vision of the Lord and clearly heard His voice saying, 'Although Communism is evil, I will open the door and no-one will shut it.' As the three hundred went out and shared the gospel, tremendous miracles began to happen. Whole towns and villages turned to Christ.

During the third period (1966–76) the government turned their attention to the Christians and sought to annihilate the underground Church. Christians were imprisoned and Bibles were burnt. Some Christians were nailed alive to the walls of churches – including Mama Kwong's own son. She says, however, that the more the persecution, the greater the glory appeared. All the three hundred 'chosen ones' determined to be faithful in proclaiming the gospel even if it meant their martyrdom. They began to preach boldly in public and many new converts were made who were invited into homes in the neighbourhood. Apparently the response was so great that every night several villages would turn to Christ. In spite of government pressure the revival spread. God confirmed His Word with signs and wonders. Even high ranking officials began to receive Christ. According to Mama Kwong, when the government decided that all Christians should be arrested, the local authorities responded, 'How can we put them all to death? There are so many. We don't have the facilities to imprison them. Besides, Christians are the best workers in our factories – we need them.'

People were healed of incurable diseases. Robbers were miraculously converted. Such was the impact that government officials began to go secretly to Christians for prayer for healing. Many turned to Christ and attended the numerous house churches throughout China.

In the fourth period (1977–1984) Christianity has spread dramatically. Reginald Klimionok reports, 'Before the persecution there were 800,000 Protestant Christians in China. In 1979 this had increased to 30 million, while in 1981 there were 50 million Christians in China. In August 1982 there was an estimated 75 million in that nation, and this has now increased to approximately 100 million Chinese Christians. Over a period of thirty years, Mama Kwong led one million people to the Lord through preaching and home cell meetings. So effective was her ministry that she was chased out of China and now lives in Japan.'

This amazing woman was imprisoned on three occasions. The third time she was in prison, Reginald Klimionok reports, 'She saw a vision. (This was in April 1974). In the vision she saw a great canal being dug. At first it was difficult for the waters to get through, but then the floods poured through them. Mama Kwong said that Christians are God's canals. The time of the greatest trials was also the time the greatest revival occurred.'

Veteran Missionary to China and Africa, Frank Holder, was in China in 1949 when the Communist forces rolled across the ancient land. He has recently been able to visit China and visit some of the areas where he served as a missionary. He says, 'The effective strength of the church is found in the now reported 400,000 house churches across the nation, such a vital force of the conservatively estimated 50 million believers. The seed has been sown at great cost in physical health, early death and untold suffering for many workers past and present.'

It is obviously impossible to be dogmatic at this time about the exact numbers of believers in China today, but the number is far higher than the ones given by the Chinese government. Dr. J. Hudson Taylor III in Toronto in 1983 said, 'Government estimates are far too low.' Reliable estimates he maintains placed their numbers from 25 to 30 million. Citing the situation in Honan province where he was born, he said that in each of 15 of the province's 111 counties, there were over 100,000 Christians – more than one and a half million in those counties alone. Careful estimates of the Christian population of Honan province, he added, placed the number at about 5 million – more than the government's estimate for all of China. Some communities reported that 70 per cent of their members were professing Christians, and Party officials complained that Communist Party members were converting.

Dr. Taylor says, 'We now have far more to learn from China than they have from us. They have learned the truth of scripture that "except a corn of wheat fall into the ground and die, it abides alone." Some of them, through incredible suffering, have learned lessons we have not.'

Even taking the lowest figure of 25 million, it shows what an amazing work of the Holy Spirit is taking place in China today.

David Wang, a Chinese born and raised in Shanghai, is the General Director of Asian Outreach. Based in Hong Kong he has travelled extensively in China and is an acknowledged expert on the Church in China. In an article in the Australian Evangel in May 1983, he wrote, 'Pastor Wang Ming Dao is called the "St. Paul of China." When I met him in 1980, he had just spent twenty-two years in prison and labour camps. He was so pleased with the amazing growth of the church and said, "This is God's handiwork. He has done great things inside China and no one else can steal His glory. We have all stood aside and could only watch and marvel. To God be the glory, great things He has done!'' The single most important factor is the supernatural power of God working miracles in answer to believing prayer.' That's revival. And as Dr. Hudson Taylor III says, 'The Chinese experience of our time is eloquent testimony that no earthly power can eliminate God's work, and truth burns brightest where the fire is hottest.'

In spite of the set back to the cause of democracy in China in 1989, with the crushing of the students in Tiananman Square, nothing can hold back the tide of revival sweeping across China. Reliable reports indicate that tens of thousands are coming to Christ every month. One statistic states that 2,600 new believers turn to the Lord every day. Of course the need for teaching and training these new believers is tremendous and the demand for sound literature and Bibles is desperate. The ageing regime remains paranoid in its fear of another student demonstration, and all foreigners remain suspect. Religious activity especially is persecuted but nevertheless the Chinese Christians themselves remain steadfast and continue to win souls without any outside help. They are proving that the power of the Holy Spirit is greater than all the power of man. In the biggest nation in the world God is still demonstrating his power.

16

The Hebrides Revival 1949

Peggy Smith was eighty-four years old and blind. Her sister Christine, two years younger, was almost doubled up with arthritis. Yet in the early hours of a winter's morning in 1949, in a little cottage near Barvas village, on the Isle of Lewis in the Scottish Hebrides, they were to be found in earnest prayer. That morning God visited them in a special way, giving them an unshakeable assurance that the revival they and others had been praying about for months, was near. Peggy (in Gaelic – their only language), told her sister, 'This is what God has promised, "I will pour water upon him that is thirsty, and floods upon the dry ground," – and we are dealing with a covenant-keeping God.'

Some months previously, Peggy had received a dream from God in which she was shown that revival was coming and the church would be crowded again with young people. At the time that seemed most unlikely. Although there had been a definite movement of the Spirit of God just before World War II, the war had taken its toll. Many left the islands to serve in the Forces or to take up other forms of war service. Some never returned, and many of those who did come back after the war, returned spiritually drained and confused. By 1949 the younger generation was drifting away from God.

After her dream, Peggy sent for her minister, James

Murray Mackay, and told him what she believed was a revelation from God. She asked him to call the church leaders to prayer. This man of God responded and for months, three nights a week, he and others met to do business with Almighty God in real prayer. His wife also had a dream in which she saw the church filled with people who were obviously concerned about their souls, and a stranger was in the pulpit.

On the same morning that God gave the two elderly sisters an assurance about the coming revival, He also drew near in a special way to the group praying with the Rev. Mackay. They had met to pray the previous night around 10 p.m. in a barn in Barvas (some 12 miles north of Stornoway). Kneeling in the straw they pleaded with Almighty God. During their praying a young deacon from the Free Church stood up and read Psalm 24: 'Who shall ascend into the hill of the Lord? Or who shall stand in His holy place? He that hath clean hands, and a pure heart; who hath not lifted up his soul unto vanity, nor sworn deceitfully.' He read the passage again and then challenged the praying group, 'Brethren, we have been praying for weeks, waiting on God. But I would like to ask now: "Are our hands clean? Is the heart pure?" ' As they continued to wait before God, His awesome presence swept into the barn. At four in the morning, in the words of Duncan Campbell, 'they moved out of the realm of the common and the natural into the sphere of the supernatural. And that is revival.'

It was Duncan Campbell of the Faith Mission that the Rev. MacKay felt led to invite to Barvas for special meetings. His leading was confirmed by Peggy Smith. She told him that, 'one night in a vision the Lord had revealed to her not only that revival was coming, but also the identity of the instrument He had chosen to use – Duncan Campbell!' (Andrew Woolsey, from his biography of Duncan Campbell).

Duncan Campbell said, 'I received a telegram in Skye,

where I was labouring, and where God was graciously moving. I replied saying that it was impossible for me to go to Lewis as I was then preparing for a convention in another parish, but I would put Lewis on my programme for the following year.' When the two praying sisters heard this, they simply said, 'That is what man has said. God has said he is coming, and he will be here within the fortnight.' Duncan Campbell related, 'I cannot go into details as to how it was necessary to cancel the convention. All I can say is that Peggy's prayer was answered and within a fortnight I was there!'

There was a great spirit of expectancy in Duncan Campbell's first meeting in the Barvas parish church (Presbyterian). A deacon declared, 'Mr. Campbell, God is hovering over. He is going to break through.' But though it was a good meeting with good singing and liberty in prayer and preaching, there was nothing more. At the end of the service, however, the same deacon told Duncan, 'Do not be discouraged; He is coming. I hear already the rumblings of heaven's chariot wheels . . .' Then he suggested to the already exceedingly travel-weary Duncan that they go and spend the night in prayer! About thirty of them retired to a nearby cottage.

Duncan Campbell described what happened, 'God was beginning to move, the heavens were opening, we were there on our faces before God. Three o'clock in the morning came, and GOD SWEPT IN. About a dozen men and women lay prostrate on the floor, speechless. Something had happened; we knew that the forces of darkness were going to be driven back, and men were going to be delivered. We left the cottage at 3 a.m. to discover men and women seeking God. I walked along a country road, and found three men on their faces, crying to God for mercy. There was a light in every home, no one seemed to think of sleep.'

When Duncan and his friends gathered at the church later in the morning, the place was crowded. A stream of buses came from every part of the island, yet no one could discover who had told them to come. A butcher in his van brought seven men from a distance of seventeen miles: all seven were gloriously converted. Now the revival was really under way. The Spirit of God was at work. All over the church men and women were crying for mercy. Some fell into a trance, some swooned, many wept.

Campbell pronounced the benediction and almost all left the chapel. Suddenly a young man began to pray. He was so burdened for the souls of his friends that he prayed for almost three-quarters of an hour. During this time the people returned to the church, joined by many others, until there were twice as many outside as inside. In some amazing way the people gathered from Stornoway, and Ness and different parishes. It was 4 a.m. the following morning before Duncan pronounced the benediction for a second time.

Even then he was still unable to go home to bed. As he was leaving the church a messenger told him, 'Mr. Campbell, people are gathered at the police station, from the other end of the parish; they are in great spiritual distress. Can anyone here come along and pray with them?' Campbell went and what a sight met him. Under the still starlit sky he found men and women on the road, others by the side of a cottage, and some behind a peat stack – all crying to God for mercy. The revival had come.

That went on for five weeks with services from early morning until late at night – or into the early hours of the morning. Then it spread to the neighbouring parishes. What had happened in Barvas was repeated over and over again. Duncan Campbell said that a feature of the revival was the overwhelming sense of the presence of God. His sacred presence was everywhere. Sinners found themselves unable to escape it. For example, a young man was witnessed to by a new convert. Suddenly conviction gripped the young man and he began to tremble. Determined to 'shake it off' he went into Stornoway and entered a pub, only to find that even in there men were talking about the salvation of their souls. He muttered, 'This is no place for me, I'll go to a dance.' He found a dance in progress but was only in the dance hall a few minutes when a young woman came up to him and mentioning his name, said, 'Oh where would eternity find us if God struck us dead now?' That evening the young man yielded his life to Christ. He could not escape from His presence.

Old Peggy and her sister enjoyed a wonderful holy intimacy with God. Andrew Woolsey relates, 'When the movement was at its height, Peggy sent for Duncan, and asked him to go to a small isolated village to hold a meeting. The people there were known to be unfavourable to the revival. Duncan explained the situation to Peggy and questioned the wisdom of her request: "Besides, I have no leading to go to that place." Peggy turned her sightless eyes in the direction of his voice. Her sightless eyes seemed to penetrate his soul: "Mr. Campbell, if you were living as near to God as you ought to be, He would reveal His secrets to you also." Duncan meekly accepted the rebuke and asked to spend the morning with them in prayer. Peggy prayed: "Lord, You remember what You told me this morning, that in this village You are going to save seven men who will become pillars in the church. Lord, I have given Your message to Mr. Campbell and it seems he is not prepared to receive it. Oh, Lord, give him wisdom, because he badly needs it!" Duncan went! He arrived there at 7 p.m. to find a large bungalow crowded to capacity, with many outside. When he finished preaching a minister beckoned him to the end of the house to speak again to a number of people who were mourning over their sins – among them, PEGGY'S SEVEN MEN!'

Confined to their cottage, Peggy and her sister

remembered each home before God, and 'they were so acquainted with the work of the Spirit that they knew instinctively where anxious souls were to be found.' The work spread throughout the Hebrides and by 1952 the *Stornoway Gazette* was able to report, 'More are attending the prayer meetings in Lewis today than attended public worship on the Sabbath before the outbreak of this revival.' Before the revival, Stornoway had one of the highest drinking rates in Scotland, and 'bothans', illegal and unlicensed drinking places, flourished. After the revival one publican moaned, 'The drink trade on the island is ruined.'

'Perhaps the greatest miracle of all was in the village of Arnol,' said Duncan Campbell. 'Here a good deal of opposition was experienced, but prayer, the mighty weapon of the revival, was resorted to and an evening given to waiting upon God. Before midnight, God "came down", the mountains flowed down at His presence, and a wave of revival swept the village. Opposition and spiritual death fled before the presence of the Lord of life. Here was demonstrated the power of prevailing prayer, and that nothing lies beyond the reach of prayer except that which lies outside the will of God. There are those in Arnol today who will bear witness to the fact that, WHILE A BROTHER PRAYED, THE VERY HOUSE SHOOK! I could only stand in silence as wave after wave of Divine power swept through the house, and in a matter of minutes following this heaven-sent visitation, men and women were on their faces in distress of soul.'

Duncan Campbell was a 'canny' Scot, a man of God of the highest integrity and not given to exaggeration. The writer well remembers being in a prayer meeting for revival in the Headquarters of the Faith Mission in Edinburgh, which he led. The room was crowded with men of spiritual quality and the writer was deeply impressed by his quiet, sincere godliness, and his aura of spiritual authority. He was clearly a chosen vessel and especially prepared by God for a very special part in the Hebridean revival.

Although the peak of the revival was between 1949 to 1952, the blessing continued to flow for many years. Even in 1957, God again manifested His power. This time, to the great delight of Duncan Campbell, it was on the island of North Uist. It was a recognised fact that Uist had never known revival. But local ministers testified that the move in Uist was even greater than the previous move in Lewis. Again the move of the Spirit of God began and was carried on by believing prayer and through faithful preaching of the Word of God. There was, however, an unusual note, for God chose as His main instruments in the Uist revival four sister pilgrims of the Faith Mission. Meetings were crowded and night after night people were found crying to God for salvation.

Some time after the visitation in Barvas, James Mac-Kay was able to write in the Christian paper *Life and Work*, 'There are more than one hundred souls in this parish whose hearts God has graciously touched since the movement started. God is maintaining them all; not one of them has gone back.'

Many young men from the revival heard the call of God and entered the ministry; others answered the call to the mission fields. 'For a while,' says Edwin Orr, 'hope was kindled in Britain by the outbreak of revival in the Scottish Hebrides under the ministry of Duncan Campbell, a movement marked by trances, visions and startling conversions; but the work did not spread to the English-speaking bulk of Scotland.'

Duncan Campbell once wrote, 'Those who seek God for revival must be prepared for God to work in His own way and not according to their programme. But His sovereignty does not relieve men of responsibility; God is the God of revival but man is the human agent through whom revival is possible. Desire for revival is one thing;

confident anticipation that our desire will be fulfilled is another.'

Can we then, in the Western world, confidently expect revival? What, if anything, can we do about it?

17

Why not Revival where I Live?

'O Holy Ghost, revival comes from Thee;
Send a revival – start the work in me:
Thy Word declares Thou will supply our need;
For blessing now, O Lord, I humbly plead.'

(Edwin Orr)

That is the last verse of the marvellous hymn by Edwin Orr, who is acknowledged by very many as being the greatest living authority on the subject of revival. That verse is probably the one that has been sung most as it has frequently been used as a chorus on its own. But if we have a genuine desire for revival in our lives and in the place where we live, then we must be willing to start with the first verse:

'Search me, O God, and know my heart today;
Try me, O Lord, and know my thoughts I pray:
See if there be some wicked way in me,
Cleanse me from ev'ry sin and set me free.'

When we ask 'Why not?' we must not be surprised if God responds with 'Why do you want revival?' That is a searching question and when the Holy Spirit begins to examine our motives it is always a very humbling experience. But then the first step to revival is always believers humbling themselves under the hand of God (I Peter 5:6).

After the outstanding author, Jamie Buckingham, had visited Paul Yonggi Cho's church inKorea, he wrote, 'In order to evaluate the Korean phenomenon we are also forced to evaluate ourselves. For one cannot ask the question 'Why?' in regards to Korea without asking 'Why not?' when it comes to the English speaking world. Most of our pastors are interested in church growth. They want to pastor a large church. The reasons behind this are varied – all the way from the boost to the uncrucified ego to the fulfilment of the command of Christ to win the lost. So far no churches that I know of have incorporated all the spiritual principles necessary to bring the spiritual results. I believe that Yonggi Cho has incorporated in his own life and the life of his church at least four spiritual principles which are bound to produce growth – quantitative as well as qualitative. These are 1) prayer, 2) utilization of women, 3) brokenness, and 4) unlimiting faith. Prayer and fasting stand at the heart of all being accomplished in Korea. After Cho's seminars in the West, pastors rush home to put the 'Jethro Principle' into practice. But small groups without the foundational emphasis in righteous living and fasting and prayer produce nothing but stacks of triplicate files and increased individualism.' (Charisma Magazine, June 1982).

However, such is the perversity of the human heart, so complex our motivations, that only God is capable of searching it and trying it. 'The heart is deceitful above all things, and desperately wicked: who can know it? I the Lord search the heart, I try the reins, even to give every man according to his ways, and according to the fruit of his doings (Jeremiah 17:9–10). The Devil sets his traps in even the most spiritual things we attempt. The writer well remembers David Duplessis telling about a zealous pastor who told him that he was going to pray and fast and would not eat again until God sent revival to his church. David told him very frankly, 'My brother, that isn't a fast – it's a hunger strike!' It is all too easy to fall into the trap of thinking, 'I have fasted for three weeks, God is bound to answer my prayers now.' The Lord Jesus warned us about that kind of heathen thinking in the Sermon on the Mount, 'The heathen think that they shall be heard for their much speaking' and, 'the hypocrites disfigure their faces, that they may appear unto men to fast' (Matthew 6:7 & 16). Our long prayers, long words and long faces may impress men, but they don't impress God. One sure sign that the Spirit of God is working in our day is that the people of God are becoming more simple and natural in their praying. 'The new birth makes the natural man spiritual, and the spiritual man natural.' The Spirit of God is removing our pretences, there is a new realism in many prayer meetings.

There are two great promises in Isaiah that every child of God who is interested in revival should cherish and heed. 'For thus saith the high and lofty One that inhabiteth eternity, whose name is Holy; I dwell in the high and holy place, with him also that is of a contrite and humble spirit, to revive the spirit of the humble, and to revive the heart of the contrite ones' (57:15). 'Thus saith the Lord . . . to this man will I look, even to him that is poor and of a contrite spirit, and trembleth at my word' (66:2). Revival starts where the Sermon on the Mount starts, with 'the poor in spirit' (Matthew 5:3).

It was the writer's privilege to be present when Edwin Orr lectured on 'The Church's Role in Revival' at a gathering of the British Church Growth Council in the Evangelical Alliance Headquarters in London, on 20th May, 1983. In his opening remarks Dr. Orr mentioned with some sadness that he observed in not a few students who went to Pasadena College to study World Missions, that they were more concerned with the techniques than the dynamics. Their attitude was wrong. The Holy Spirit is the great dynamic force behind every revival. It is a misnomer to call an evangelistic crusade a revival.

Dr. Orr went on to emphasise that revival cannot be organised; there is no technique that can guarantee revival. This is where he begs to differ with the famed revivalist Charles Finney. Finney's concept, says Dr. Orr, 'is that revival is nothing more than the right use of the appropriate means . . . revival is something for man to do.' In his lectures, Finney likens revival to a farmer and a guaranteed crop, '. . . a revival is as naturally a result of the use of the appropriate means as a crop is of the use of its appropriate means.' Dr. Orr stressed that Finney's success was due to the fact that Finney was labouring in a time of revival.

In his invaluable little book *The Re-Study of Revival and Revivalism* published in 1981, Dr. Orr says, '. . . Finney's theories have not always worked in times of spiritual decline, when there was lacking any spirit of revival. Unfortunately, besides inspiring countless local pastors and evangelists to seek revival, Finney's theory brought about a school of brash evangelists who fancied that they could produce revival anywhere with means selected by themselves at times decided by themselves. True, the use of means by motivated men of God was usually productive, but such use of means by worldly operators soon produced promotional evangelism, manipulated and sensationalized, commercialized and exploited. It has been demonstrated that a local church obediently responding to the light already given will surely come to know a measure of revival locally. But such limited events are seldom likely to provoke a nationwide awakening, even though the localized revival may continue for a lengthy time, and produce a fellowship of churches.'

Finney clearly swung the pendulum too far in his reaction against the fatalism that had well nigh paralysed his denomination at that time. The great awakenings of

1739; 1857–59; 1904–5; and the like, were not planned, programmed or promoted. 'It must therefore be concluded,' says Edwin Orr, 'that Finney's principles applied to local efforts of renewal or evangelism rather than to widespread movements of the Holy Spirit.'

Through the cross, God has eternally demonstrated that He will never allow any flesh to glory in His presence (I Cor 1:29). That was the significance of Evan Roberts' prayer when he cried, 'Bend me! Bend me!' Evan Roberts confessed, 'What "bent" me was God commending His love and my not seeing anything in it to commend.' Through a revelation of Calvary love by the Holy Spirit his heart was melted and broken. The whole theme of the revival was Christ's Calvary love. It is safe to say that there has never been a revival without the believers first being broken. 'The sacrifices of God are a broken spirit: a broken and a contrite heart, O God, thou wilt not despise' (Psalm 51:17). A fresh revelation of the Cross and all that it meant to the Christ of God 'to be made sin for us, Who knew no sin' (2 Cor 5:21) is a pre-requisite for revival. Indeed, when we truly begin to 'survey the wondrous cross, on which the Prince of Glory died,' then we do not say, 'Why not where I live?' But, with Evan Roberts we see that there is nothing in us at all to warrant such love. We no longer say 'Why not?' but rather 'Why ever should God bless us with revival?' Only when we come to the end of ourselves do we come to the beginning of God and the realisation that it is all, like salvation, of His grace and His mercy. A Moravian historian writing of the days prior to the culminating day of 13th August, 1797 says, 'Every one desired above everything else that the Holy Spirit might have full control. Self-love and self-will, as well as all disobedience, disappeared, and an overwhelming flood of grace swept us all out into the great ocean of Divine love.'

As soon as we know that we are right with God, that our relationship is restored and renewed, it is certain that we shall become very sensitive about our relationship with other believers. Again and again throughout those high days of the Welsh Revival, Evan Roberts would ask, 'Have you forgiven everybody, everybody, EVERYBODY? If not, don't expect forgiveness for your own sins. You won't get it.'

Balance is essential in all spiritual matters, but never more so than concerning revival. William Sprague in his *Lectures on Revivals of Religion* (which Dr. Martin Lloyd-Jones described as 'The outstanding classic on this vital and important matter,') says, 'It is possible to attribute to the Spirit too little agency, and too much, in revivals of religion. There are those on the one hand who attribute too little to this Almighty Agent. They speak of revivals as if they were produced altogether by man; and if the Spirit is mentioned at all, it is in a way that would indicate that He had little to do with it. On the other hand, there are those who attribute too much to the agency of the Spirit. They do this who speak of revivals as if God only was at work in them, and man a mere passive recipient of impressions. We honour the Holy Spirit most, when we give Him precisely the place which he claims; when we recognise Him as the efficient author of conviction, conversion, and sanctification; but He is offended when we undertake to palm upon Him what we ought to take with shame to ourselves.'

In his memoirs of the Azusa Street Revival in Los Angeles in 1906, (one of the focal points for the beginning of the Pentecostal Movement this century) Frank Bartleman says, 'God broke strong men and women to pieces and put them together again for His glory. It was a tremendous overhauling process. Pride, self-assertion, self-importance, and self-esteem could not survive there.

'Presumptuous men would sometimes come among us. Especially preachers with their self-opinions. But their efforts were short-lived. They generally bit the dust in humility going through the process we had all gone through. In other words, they died out, came to see themselves in all their weakness, then in childlike humility and confession were taken up of God and transformed through the mighty baptism of the Holy Spirit.'

If we are willing to let God take us apart and put us together again, then we may well find that God will answer our 'Why not revival where I live?' with His 'Why not indeed!'

18

What are the Conditions for Revival?

'Nothing messes up cemeteries like resurrections,' says Jack Hayford, the well know pastor of Church on the Way in California. The first condition for revival is that we must be prepared for our dead churches and dull ministries to be drastically disturbed by an inflow of divine life. The words used for revival in the Old Testament mean, 'restore, renew or repair;' and 'revive or bring back to life'. In essence the words apply to believers, for spiritually speaking, unbelievers are 'dead in trespasses and sins' (Ephesians 2:1). However, if we are honest we have to admit that when the Church is at a low ebb, it is hard to tell the difference between the two. In the parable of the good Samaritan the 'man who went down from Jerusalem to Jericho and fell among thieves' could well represent the backslider, or the Christian who has become cold of heart, in so far as he was described as 'half dead' (Lk 10:30). In the parable of the prodigal son, the younger brother is described as 'dead' (Luke 15:32). In defining terms, it is well to bear in mind these vital distinctions that 'revival' pertains to believers, and 'awakening' to the unbelieving community around the Church. Revival is God by His Spirit bringing back to full and vigorous health His 'half-dead' people. Awakening then follows as God by His Spirit prepares the unregenerate masses to respond to the anointed proclamation of the gospel by the revived Church. On the day of Pentecost, Peter quoted Joel's prophecy to explain what was happening, 'And it shall come to pass in the last days, saith God, I will pour out of my Spirit upon all flesh . . .' (Acts 2:17). It is instructive to notice that Peter's very full quotation from Joel (2:28–32) makes it clear that the outpouring of the Spirit is on the whole body of believers (sons and daughters, young and old, servants and handmaidens), and will so affect the unregenerate community that many of them will be awakened to 'call upon the name of the Lord and be saved.' In that sense 'the outpouring of God's Spirit' is a comprehensive phrase which covers both revival and awakening. It is significant that in the eighteenth and nineteenth centuries Christians frequently used this expression in their prayers. In this twentieth century the phrase has not been used so much and the emphasis has more and more been placed upon the infilling of individuals.

Nothing messes up cemeteries like resurrections, and nothing disturbs our cosy little Christian huddles like an outpouring of the Spirit. In the early days of the Pentecostal Movement in Britain there was a period when many of the little groups of newly filled believers were in danger of 'turning in on themselves'. Finding themselves ostracised for their 'tongues speaking', many became nothing more than little holy clubs where believers enjoyed themselves exercising the various gifts of the Spirit. As Donald Gee says in his history of the Pentecostal Movement, 'During 1925, Smith Wigglesworth conducted some useful and powerful campaigns in Great Britain. They helped to pave the way for much larger campaigns to follow. Some of the assemblies had remained small and semi-private for so long that they felt quite embarrassed at the limelight which bolder methods of proclaiming their testimony soon occasioned.' The Charismatic Renewal passed through similar phases when for many it was a cosy little group in the vestry or the vicarage. The House Church Movement has also been in danger of the same overemphasis on separation, resulting in some becoming smugly satisfied in their happy little groups. Fortunately God raised up men and women of vision and passion and courage in the Pentecostal Movement, such as George and Stephen Jeffreys, and John Nelson Parr, and Aimée Semple McPherson, who realised that the primary purpose of the baptism of the Holy Spirit was an enduement of power to witness to the glorified and risen Christ. Wherever the Pentecostals have kept evangelistic they have kept healthy and have prospered. In the last few years it has been good to see God raising up leadership within the Charismatic Movement such as David Watson and Colin Urquhart who have swept aside the 'holy remnant' mentality and moved the ever growing army of Charismatics of all denominations into a 'holy war' attitude! The same applies to the House Church Movement; God has raised up leaders within their ranks who have realised the dangers of becoming too introspective and they are now moving out into evangelism. The prospects are thrilling for the Kingdom of God, but watch out Satan and hosts of darkness! The Spirit of God is moving and all the different ranks are beginning to march to the same tune and sing the same song, because there is one Lord, and one Body, and one Spirit.

'History reveals that evangelism alone seldom results in revival, but revival always produces evangelism,' states Mrs. Vonette Bright, who chairs the Lausanne Committee's Intercession Advisory Group.

An indispensable condition for revival is that we must be prepared for God to work in any way He chooses. We must be willing for all our plans to be laid on the altar. There is no escaping the cross, either in regeneration or in revival. The cross will always confront saints as well as sinners. Peter found this to his cost. No sooner had he been blessed with the Father's revelation to him that Jesus was 'the Christ, the Son of the living God,' (Matthew 16:16), than he found himself arguing with Jesus over the cross (v 21). 'Then Peter took Jesus, and began to rebuke him, saying Be it far from thee Lord: this shall not be unto thee' (v 22). The Greek literally is 'Pity thyself'. Self-pity is one of the most subtle forms of self. The Lord immediately recognised its source (v 23) and rejected it. In doing so He reminded Peter and all His followers of the necessity of taking up the cross daily (v 24). Revival may well cost us our position, our leadership, our security, our reputation. It is a law of the Kingdom: 'Whosoever will save his life shall lose it: and whosoever will lose his life for my sake shall find it.' (v 25).

In every revival there is a breaking down of denominationalism. It is only afterwards when things begin to settle down that men build the walls that separate believers. The great Scottish evangelist, James A. Stewart (who was so greatly used of God in revivals in Europe in the 1930s), writing of the Welsh revival says, 'One of the most significant results was that the old church prejudices were broken down. The man-made denominational barriers completely collapsed as believers and pastors of all denominations worshipped their majestic Lord together. The quarrels of local Christians were healed. One of the outstanding features of the revival was the confession of sin, not among the unsaved alone, but among the saved. All were broken down and melted before the cross of Christ.'

This has been a feature of many revivals. Edwin Orr says of the awakening at the beginning of the twentieth century, 'It was most significant that the Awakening of the 1900s was ecumenical, in the best senses of the word. It was thoroughly interdenominational: Anglican, Baptist, Brethren, Congregational, Disciple, Lutheran, Methodist, Presbyterian and Reformed congregations sharing in the revival.'

175

Another vital condition for revival is an awareness of God's time. Ralph Mahoney, the founder of World Missionary Assistance Plan, has had the unique privilege of ministry-related travel in over one hundred countries of the world. Over the past thirty-four years he has participated in great revival movements in Africa, Asia, Latin America, and the Western world. The writer has counted it a great privilege to have had fellowship with this Spirit-filled servant of God and to attend several of his seminars. Ralph Mahoney says that the following has been his continual prayer for about twenty years: 'Lord, let me be a son of Issachar. Give me the capacity to have an understanding of what You are doing, of Your times and seasons, so I can co-operate and flow with what You are doing.' (I Chronicles 12:32 tells us: 'The sons of Issachar were men that had understanding of the times to know what Israel ought to do.') That is a wise prayer.

Paul obviously had this God-given sensitivity to the leading of the Spirit concerning God's timing. In Acts 16 we read that 'they were forbidden of the Holy Ghost to preach the word in Asia' (v 6). God also closed the door when they tried to go into Bithynia (v 7). Then came the vision which took them to Philippi (v 9) and although they were put in prison, they finished up with revival and succeeded in planting a New Testament church. It should also be observed that a few short years later, Paul found himself in Ephesus when it was God's time for Asia, for in his two years at Ephesus, God sent such a great revival 'that all they which dwelt in Asia heard the word of the Lord Jesus, both Jews and Greeks.' (Acts 19:10).

There is a significant promise in Zechariah 10:1, 'Ask ye of the Lord rain in the time of the latter rain; so the Lord shall make bright clouds, and give them showers of rain.' The former rain is the November rain which falls after the ingathering of the autumn harvest. Without this rain the ground remains too hard to plough. The former rain softens the earth for ploughing and planting. The latter rain (which some estimate to be about seven times greater) falls in spring and summer to bring the grain to maturity and ripening in readiness for the great autumn harvest.

It is always right to seek to win souls and to witness, at all times, 'in season and out of season' (2 Timothy 4:2). Equally, we must always be engaged in prayer, indeed we are exhorted to 'pray without ceasing' (I Thessalonians 5:17). There will always be some measure of blessing, always some response to the faithful preaching of God's word. But it is rather like strawberries. One can always obtain fresh strawberries all the year round, provided one is prepared to pay the price when they are out of season. That is not the time when wise housewives make their strawberry jam! They wait until strawberries are in season. Then they can go to the strawberry fields and gather them by the bucketful at a very low price.

Britain has been 'out of season' for a long period. Many have despaired of revival ever coming to this land again. America, on the other hand, has enjoyed some measure of revival blessing in the post war era. However, there is a growing conviction among men and women of the Spirit that we are at last moving into God's time for an outpouring of the Spirit upon Britain and America. When God speaks, He never leaves us with just one witness, it is a divine principle that every word shall be established by two or three witnesses (2 Corinthians 13:1). Furthermore, God always chooses reliable and proven witnesses when He wishes to reveal something to His people. It is therefore very thrilling to find so many voices saying the same thing – namely that God's time for revival is at hand.

Witness number one is the Rev. Henry Brash Bonsall, M.A., B.D., the highly respected Principal of the Birmingham Bible Institute. In the Winter issue of the College Magazine *Gateway*, he wrote, 'We as a College are poised in preparation for the Revival which God showed me fifty years ago He was going to send to this country. In this Revival, He has revealed, it is not so much religious people that will be converted but leaders in industry, professional life, political life, and experts. These will be people who have never darkened a church door and have not the scintilla of an idea of what Christ really is. To such He will be revealed. Revival means God coming to a community face-to-face when the hearts of hardest rock will flow down like lava, and men will be called to be God's servants to the ends of the earth. They will come to this, and every available college, demanding instant training.'

Just before his death on the 17th March 1978, Len Moules, former secretary of the World Evangelisation Crusade (founded by C. T. Studd), wrote, 'Of the 210 countries which constitute the world scene, the stirrings of revival have now touched well over 70 countries since 1960. Behind the Iron and Bamboo curtains the Spirit of God is moving significantly. This is but the beginning. God will pour His Spirit out on all flesh. We shall see the Spirit poured out upon the Muslims, and Isaac will be more important than Ishmael, and Jesus as Saviour rather than their own prophet. The Buddhists under the Spirit's touch will find Jesus to be the Way, the Truth and the Life. "The four-fold way and eight-fold path" will yield to the One above all others. Upon Confucian thought and "the dark and light principles" will come the revelation of Jesus Who said, "I am the light of the world." What exciting days! Be ready, be praying, be expectant and thankful for revival that is at our door. Hallelujah.' Len Moules was one of the most experienced and trusted missionary statesmen of our day.

When the writer was privileged to interview Reinhard Bonnke in 1979, and talk with him about revival, here are some of the things he said, 'God seems to have His times of harvest for the various parts of the world. Once it was Indonesia and South Korea, then South America or South Africa, then it will be Europe, it will be Britain and I am absolutely convinced in my heart that God's time for Britain is approaching and God's time for Germany is approaching very fast. As sure as the sun is shining – God is going to pour out His Spirit on these isles.'

When the writer talked with Yonggi Cho in 1981 he said, 'I really do believe that something great is going to happen throughout the land of Great Britain.'

It is God's time and those who really believe this will be praying and preparing, not sitting back and doing nothing. Even in the time of the latter rain, we are to 'ask for rain' says the prophet Zechariah.

At the Charismatic leaders' conference in December 1983, Arthur Wallis, the well-known author of *In The Day of Thy Power*, (and what is in essence a more up to date version of that book, *Rain From Heaven*), told the writer that he felt that God had been speaking to him and telling him to 'take the subject of revival off the back-burner'. In other words, after years of patient waiting and praying, the indications are that we are now coming into God's time for revival.

In talking with Yonggi Cho in 1981, the writer asked him about preparing for revival, and received this wise advice, 'Preparation for revival is like building a dam ahead of the rain. Even though we really desire a downpour to quench the drought, if we don't build a dam, we shall not keep that rain. If God showers down revival and individual ministers and churches are not ready to accept it, then all the blessings of the revival will be wasted. Therefore I say it is the hour for Great Britain to train the ministers and lay Christians to be ready to accept this revival.'

Len Moules warned that there are many lessons to be learned from the recent revivals around the world. 'Primarily it is the fact that God will pour out His Spirit when He wills, and through whom He wills. The manifestations of His outpourings are varied according to the will of the Reviver. Of it all we must say that God is greater and bigger than all our concepts of revival. We must learn to accept Him through whoever He comes, and with whatever accompanying manifestations.' That is especially important, for most of the recent revivals have been accompanied by signs and wonders and miracles and the gifts of the Spirit as detailed in I Corinthians 12. Edwin Orr, speaking of the second great awakening which began in the industrial cities of Yorkshire in late 1791, says, 'It spread to the rural areas of Britain, cresting among the Methodists who seemed unafraid of the phenomena of mass awakening.' Always of course, every manifestation must be tested by the Word of God, and by the acknowledgement of the Incarnate Son of God (Isaiah 8:19-20; I John 4:1-3). But the people of God must not be afraid of mighty demonstrations of God's power in supernatural ways.

Duncan Campbell in speaking of Hebridean revival gave these words of wisdom, 'Physical manifestations and prostrations have been a further feature. I find it somewhat difficult to explain this aspect, indeed I cannot; but this I will say, that the person who would associate this with satanic influence is coming perilously near committing the unpardonable sin. Lady Huntingdon on one occasion wrote to George Whitefield respecting cases of crying out and falling down in meetings, and advised him not to remove them from the meetings as he had done. When this is done it seemed to bring a damper on the meeting. She said: "You are making a great mistake. Don't be wiser than God. Let them cry out; it will do a great deal more good than your preaching." '

Ralph Mahoney out of his wide experience also wisely advises, 'I've observed that in the pathway to revival or blessing, God puts a stone of stumbling so that the proud and insincere have an excuse to reject His visitation. God gives religious people a good excuse to stumble at what He's doing. You can miss God's visitation because of your preconceptions. I know people who have prayed for years that God would send revival, and when it came, they rejected it. Why? Speaking in tongues accompanied it. "I can't accept it because they don't allow that in my denomination." Speaking in tongues was the stone of stumbling, the rock of offence.'

Coming back to the pattern for all revivals, the book of Acts, although Christ had promised that He would send the Spirit, the obedient one hundred and twenty, 'all continued with one accord in prayer and supplication' (Acts 1:14). That continued for ten days, and 'when the day of Pentecost was fully come, they were all with one accord in one place' (2:1). With the result that 'they were all filled with the Holy Ghost' and 'three thousand were added to the church' (2:4, 41).

E. J. Poole-Connor in his classic work *Evangelicalism in England* gives his considered opinion that, 'Our anticipation, then, based upon these and other Scriptures, is that while the close of the age will witness grievous declension, it will be broken in upon, ere judgment falls, by a powerful world-wide testimony to the grace of God; and that this testimony will be accompanied by a great work of the Holy Spirit which will complete the fulfilment of the prophecy of Joel. But inasmuch as such visitations of grace have always been associated with Evangelical preaching, it behoves those who desire to be granted some share therein to acquaint themselves speedily with the Evangelical gospel, and to range themselves clearly and whole-heartedly under its banner.'

There is an expectation, which is not without foundation, that the coming revival will be the greatest revival of them all. As Edwin Orr has observed, 'The Reformers were more evangelical than the Lollards, the Puritans were more evangelical than the Reformers, and the Revivalists of the 18th century were more zealous for soul-winning than the Puritans, whilst those of the 19th were much more enterprising than forerunners in the 18th; and ecumenists have conceded that 20th century Pentecostalists outdo older denominations in zeal.' In other words, every awakening has made the Church more radically New Testament in character.

Southern Baptist American television and crusade evangelist, James Robison, wrote recently after undergoing a great spiritual release in his ministry, 'I believe the greatest revival in the history of the Church is on its way. Everywhere I go I see new, dramatic unmistakable evidence of the awesome work of preparation now being carried out by the Holy Spirit. Like a mighty tidal wave, this revival is now rising in majesty many miles from shore. Soon – only God knows when – it will come thundering inland. And in its wake, countless lives will be forever changed.'

A leading British voice to say a similar thing is the author of the amazingly popular daily Bible readings *Every Day With Jesus*. At the beginning of 1984, Selwyn Hughes, wrote, 'In the forty years that I have been a Christian I have never witnessed such a burden and expectancy for revival as I do at this moment among the true people of God. Wherever I go I meet prayerful Christians whose spirit witnesses with my own that a mighty Holy Spirit revival is on the way. Slowly but surely their faith is rising to flashpoint.'

The question is, will we be a part of the coming revival or will we fight it, as many did in the past with previous revivals? We are almost at the flashpoint. We must prepare the way of the Lord by humbling ourselves under the mighty hand of God. We must give ourselves to seeking Him in fervent prayer. We must open our hearts and our minds to be ready for the coming visitation when God pours out His Spirit as floods upon the dry ground. We must realise that revival comes 'Not by might, nor by power, but by My Spirit, saith the Lord of Hosts' (Zechariah 4:6).

19

Will We Recognise Revival When It Comes?

Standing at the brink of the last decade of this convulsive century I am more certain than ever that Revival is coming. When the first edition of this book was published in 1984, Revival was not a particularly popular topic. The year 1990 dawned with Revival being written about, talked about, and prayed for, everywhere. There is no question at all in my mind but that the revival already bursting forth in country after country will prove to be the most far reaching revival of all time. It will be the greatest demonstration of God's power with signs, wonders, miracles and gifts of the Holy Spirit. It will be of global dimensions, affecting every part of the world.

It will also be a most searching time for the Church. New discoveries of God's power will of necessity be matched by new disclosures and acceptance of God's undiminished holiness, which in turn will provoke bitter opposition from the world and result in violent onslaughts by Satan. Revival is not a soft option. The highly respected missions research analyst, David B. Barrett, reports the increase of Christian martyrs: 'The annual numbers of martyrs involved throughout the twentieth century are far higher than any of us had hitherto imagined. Martyrdom continues to play a major role in local, national, regional, and global evangelisation.' Barrett estimates that by the year 2000 the number of Christians killed because of their faith in Christ will increase to half a million annually. He defines martyrdom as 'losing one's life for Christ as a result of human hostility'.

These statistics make some of the obscure verses in Revelation seem suddenly very relevant: 'And when he had opened the fifth seal, I saw under the altar the souls of them that were slain for the word of God, and for the testimony which they held; And they cried with a loud voice, saying, How long, O Lord, holy and true, dost thou not judge and avenge our blood on them that dwell on the earth? and white robes were given unto every one of them; and it was said unto them, that they should rest yet for a little season, until their fellow servants also and their brethren, that should be killed as they were, should be fulfilled' (Revelation 6:9–11). Professor W. J. Hollenweger, modern church historian and noted author, says: 'Evangelism is the most dangerous business.' It is more so in revival not less, as the Church's first martyr, Stephen, quickly discovered. Being full of faith and power, Stephen 'did great wonders and miracles among the people . . . and they were not able to resist the wisdom and the spirit by which he spake' but they still stoned him to death (Acts 6:8, 10).

The last decade of this century is set for the introduction of widespread changes in all areas of life, spiritual as well as secular. Tom Sine, who is described as a creative consultant, predicts that we will experience as much change in the next ten years as we have in the past three decades. (17 November, 1989 in *Christianity Today*). Like it or not, the Church is already undergoing drastic changes and it can no more prevent them than could King Canute halt the tide. For example, church statisticians inform us that in 1980 the number of non-white Christians surpassed the number of whites for the first time in history. Britain with its Anglicanism and France with its Catholicism can no longer be realistically regarded as Christian societies.

It is tragically true that they, along with the rest of Europe, are now being classed as mission fields ripe for evangelisation. Missionary stateman Paul E. Kauffman, affirms: 'The Third World is where the revival fires are burning most brightly and where the Church is growing most rapidly. Soon, the Third World will be home to seventy per cent of the world's evangelicals. They will become the dominant force in Christendom in the Decade of the Nineties, not only because of their sheer numbers, but because of the spiritual dynamism found in their churches.'

Modern church historian Professor Vinsan Synan takes a similar view. 'It is altogether possible that the future of Christianity will be moulded by the developing Third-World, indigenous pentecostal churches interreacting with the vigorous charismatic elements in the traditional churches. The recent history of church growth in Africa and Latin America indicates that Christian affairs of the twenty-first century may well be largely in the hands of the Third World and a resurgent Roman Catholicism inspired and renewed by the charismatic renewal.'

That is a humbling thought for the Western Church, but it has happened before. The Church was still in its infancy when God in his over-ruling providence, to all intents and purposes, shifted the centre of missionary outreach from Jerusalem to Antioch. However, humility is always a pre-requisite to revival, and if we in the affluent West are willing to 'humble ourselves under the mighty hand of God' and learn from the 'poor Christians in the Third World, who are rich in faith', we may be in a position to recognise and receive the revival when it comes.

And come it will, for God always fulfils His promises. Hitherto there have been partial fulfilments of His promise 'to pour out His Spirit upon all flesh' (Acts 2:17) but soon He will fill it to the full. The Gospel will be fully preached to all, leaving no one with the excuse that they never heard the Gospel convincingly presented. Paul's claim that 'through mighty signs and wonders, by the power of the Spirit of God, from Jerusalem to Illyricum he had fully preached the Gospel of Christ' (Romans 15:19), will be applicable to every part of this planet.

The question is, shall we be willing to receive God's message if the messengers he sends are black, brown, or yellow? We may want to dismiss out of hand the very idea that a God-sent revival could come our way and we would not recognise it, but think again. Remember the telling parable of Jesus about children playacting weddings and funerals in the marketplace. Some children just would not play, no matter what game their friends suggested. A wedding was too happy for them and a funeral was too solemn for them. It was Jesus's telling way of reminding the Jewish leaders, the Pharisees and the lawyers, that they were behaving just like spoiled children. Nothing God did suited them. He had sent John the Baptist, as strait-laced and solemn as any funeral, and they rejected him and went so far as to say he had a devil. God sent his Son as a happy bridegroom inviting everyone to his wedding feast, and they said he was much too joyful and friendly to be the Messiah (Luke 7:29–35). The Holy Spirit, the Comforter, has been well described as 'Jesus's other self', which seems permissible in the light of John 14:16, 'I will pray the Father and he will give you another Comforter . . .'. The word used for 'another' signifies another of the same kind, not another of a different kind.

If Christ could come to his own and not be received, we should not presume that the Holy Spirit could never be treated in the same way. It is all too easy to slip into what might be termed 'the Naaman syndrome', Naaman so nearly missed being healed of his leprosy because of his mind fixation. This great Syrian general went off in a huff because Elisha did not do it 'his way'. Naaman raged: 'Behold, I thought, he will surely come out to me, and stand, and call on the name of the LORD his God, and strike his hand over the place, and recover the leper'

(II Kings 5:11). Fortunately for Naaman he was a big enough man to listen to the wise reasoning of his servants. He repented, because what is repentance but a change of mind leading to right action? He accepted that although River Abana and River Pharpar were nicer rivers than the Jordan, it was this one which God had chosen to use.

Even the saintly Andrew Murray nearly missed out when God sent revival to his own congregation. At first he was in danger of mistaking the movings of God's Spirit as fleshly anarchy. Subsequently, like Naaman, after second thoughts he realised that behind the noise and screaming, what he was witnessing was tremendous conviction of sin as a result of the working of the Holy Spirit in the hearts of his people. Visitations of God have frequently caused offence and misunderstanding.

There have been genuine revivals in which weeping, mourning, prostrations and confessions of sins have been the main features; there have been equally genuine visitations of the Almighty in which joy, praise, singing and even dancing have been the prominent manifestations. The working of the Spirit cannot be stereotyped. 'There are diversities of [the Spirit's] operations, but it is the same God which worketh all in all' (I Corinthians 12:6). May it never have to be said of us in the West, 'You stiffnecked and uncircumcised in heart and ears, you do always resist the Holy Spirit: as your fathers did, so do you' (Acts 7:51).

If we are not going to miss revival, then we must keep our hearts tender. 'As the Holy Spirit saith, Today, if you will hear his voice, harden not your hearts' (Hebrews 3:7, 8). The Spirit, like the Saviour, frequently comes to us in such graciousness and gentle humility, that we cannot believe it is really him, and we grieve him, or quench him with our arrogance, our self-sufficiency, and our proud intellectualism. It is all too easy to do 'despite unto the Spirit of grace'. Or, as the NIV renders it, 'to insult the Spirit of grace' (Hebrews 10:29).

As John the Baptist languished in prison it seems clear

that even he, who had been the subject of the clearest of prophecies and whose birth had been heralded by the most wonderful promises, was experiencing an attack of the darkest doubts. He despatched two of his faithful disciples to Jesus with the double question: 'Art thou he that should come? or look we for another?' (Luke 7:19). Can this possibly be the same one who just a few months before had stood on the banks of the Jordan and declared: 'I saw the Spirit descending from heaven like a dove, and it abode upon him. And I knew him not: but he that sent me to baptize with water, the same said unto me, Upon whom thou shalt see the Spirit descending, and remaining on him, the same is he which baptizeth with the Holy Spirit. And I saw and bare record that this is the Son of God'?

How graciously, tenderly and effectively did the Master deal with his doubting forerunner. The answer of Jesus was to make the blind see, the lame walk, to cleanse lepers from their loathsome disease, to give the deaf their hearing, and even to raise the dead. Having done that he told the two messengers: 'Go and tell John what things you have seen and heard.' Then he added this little personal postscript, and tell him, 'Blessed is he, whosoever shall not be offended in me' (v. 23).

That little postscript by Jesus was quickened to me in a special way very early in my ministry when I was tempted to question the working of the Holy Spirit. It has saved me again and again from being offended by God's dealings in my life or from taking offence over the attitudes of men. Even after experiencing genuine manifestations of God's power in revival, such is the deceitfulness of the human heart that on a bad day we may question: 'Is this the revival that should come? or are we still looking for another?'

The recent downfalls of not a few prominent figures in the charismatic and evangelical world should serve to remind all believers of the urgent necessity to 'take heed lest we fall'. The fact that we belong to a so-called revival movement is no guarantee in itself of continuing revival or of being the instrument of coming revival. If we ever allow ourselves to become proud of our position or our denomination we can be sure that God will take it upon himself to resist us, because he has put it on record that he 'resisteth the proud but giveth grace unto the humble' (James 4:6).

If the Holy Spirit can find people in any section of the Church, Catholic or Protestant, who will humble themselves, it is clear that he will visit them and raise them up. As one brought up a 'die-hard Protestant' I have struggled – and still struggle – with the thorny question as to how God can possibly bless Catholics with the blessing of the Holy Spirit and revival. I can only say that God has made me see that he does not bless either Protestantism or Cathlicism as systems. Within both the systems there are extremes which are unacceptable. There are some so-called Protestants whose mindset does not allow them to alter their tradition one iota. On the other hand there is a small but significant number of Catholics who are daring to break with centuries of tradition and risk all to search the scriptures and seek for the Spirit and his gifts in their quest for revival. There are too many Protestants who deny the very basic fundamentals of the Faith, such as the Virgin Birth and the Physical Resurrection of Christ, whereas most Catholics hold to these truths without wavering, and are open to the miraculous and God's supernatural working today. God looks at our hearts not our labels. I can only say: 'Who is sufficient for these things?' and pray that God will keep me from ever accepting what is not of him, or from ever denying what is of him.

It is, alas, all too readily conceivable that even the best of men may fail. It is also not difficult to conceive that even the best of churches and traditions may falter and fail. But, it is absolutely inconceivable that the Holy Spirit of God could or will fail. The Son of God declared with ringing certainty, 'When the Comforter is come, whom I will send unto you from the Father, even the Spirit of truth, which proceedeth from the Father, he shall testify of me' (John 15:26). Twenty-first century man will find, as did first-century man, that there is no escaping a confrontation with God's Christ – either in this life or the next. 'For to this end Christ both died, and rose, and revived that he might be Lord both of the dead and living' (Romans 14:9).

In essence Revival is the Holy Spirit testifying of the reality of Jesus, through him being afforded his rightful place of Lord and Christ in the local church. The benefits of his kingdom and rule are in turn fully demonstrated to all the inhabitants throughout that locality. None are allowed to escape the eternal question: 'Will you have this man to reign over you?'

Surely that is precisely what happened in the great revival in Asia Minor so graphically described for us by Doctor Luke in Acts 20. Paul's anointed ministry in Ephesus continued for two years, 'so that all they which dwelt in Asia heard the word of the Lord Jesus, both Jews and Greeks. And God wrought special miracles by the hands of Paul; so that from his body were brought unto the sick handkerchiefs or aprons, and the diseases departed from them, and the evil spirits went out of them.' This was power evangelism escalating into full blown revival so that 'the name of the Lord Jesus was magnified' (v. 18) and 'the word of God grew mightily and prevailed' (v. 20) – against all opposition of men and demons.

The cry of our hearts is: 'Lord, do it again in our day that this generation may not pass without Jesus Christ being clearly portrayed as crucified before their very eyes' (Galatians 3:1). That is the purpose of revival: to reveal the Lord Jesus Christ in all his saving glory that men, women and children in every country may believe in him as Saviour and crown him Lord of every part of their lives.

Bibliography

Chapter 1 The Fourth 'R'

Preaching and Preachers by D. Martin Lloyd-Jones. Hodder and Stoughton (1971 Edition).
Evangelicalism in England by E. J. Poole-Connor. Henry E. Walter Ltd. (1966 Edition).
Men of God by Oswald J. Smith. Marshall Morgan and Scott (1971 Edition).
The Fervent Prayer by J. Edwin Orr. Moody Press, Chicago (1974 Edition).
Revival Year Sermons by C. H. Spurgeon. Banner of Truth Trust (1959 Edition).
The Second Evangelical Awakening in Britain by J. Edwin Orr. Marshall Morgan and Scott (1953 Edition).

Chapter 2 1734 – New England

Jonathan Edwards: Basic Writings Selected, Edited and with a Foreword, by Ola Elizabeth Winslow. The New English Library Ltd. (A Signet Classic from New American Library) (1966 Edition).
The Inextinguishable Blaze by A. Skevington Wood. Paternoster Press (1967 Edition).
Pioneers of Revival by Charles Clarke. Fountain Trust (1971).
The Great Awakening by Joseph Tracy. Banner of Truth Trust (1976).

Chapter 3 1735–Wales: Howell Harris and Daniel Rowlands

The Christian Leaders of England In the Eighteenth Century by John Charles Ryle. Chas. J. Thynne & Jarvis, Ltd. (1868).

The Romance of Nonconformity by Joseph Ritson. W. A. Hammond (1910).

The Inextinguishable Blaze by A. Skevington Wood. Paternoster Press (1960).

Evangelicalism in England by E. J. Poole-Connor. Henry E. Walter Ltd. (1951).

Chapter 4 England 1739: George Whitefield and John Wesley

The Inextinguishable Blaze by A. Skevington Wood. Paternoster Press (1960).

George Whitefield by Arnold Dallimore. Banner of Truth Trust (1970).

The History of Revivals by William E. Allen. Revival Publishing Co. (1951).

The Christian Leaders of England in the Eighteenth Centry by J. C. Ryle. Chas. J. Thynne & Jarvis, Ltd. (1868).

Evangelicalism in England by E. J. Poole-Connor. Henry E. Walter Ltd. (1951).

Whitefield's Journals Banner of Truth Trust (1960).

Wesley's Journal (Abridged by Percy Livingstone Parker). Isbister & Company Ltd. (1902).

The Great Awakening by Joseph Tracy. Banner of Truth Trust (1976).

George Whitefield And the Great Awakening by John Pollock. Lion Publishing (Paperback Edition 1982).

The Light of the Nations by J. Edwin Orr. Paternoster Press (1965).

The Burning Heart — John Wesley: Evangelist by A. Skevington Wood. Paternoster Press (1967).

Chapter 5 The Ranters' Revival 1800–30. Hugh Bourne and William Clowes

The Romance of Nonconformity by Joseph Ritson. W. A. Hammond (1910).

A Methodist Pageant by B. Aquila Barber. Holborn Publishing House (1932).

History of the Primitive Methodist Connexion by H. B. Kendall. Joseph Toulson (1889).

The Earnest Preacher — Memories of the Rev. J. Spoor compiled by E. Hall. Joseph Toulson (1870).

The Pilgrim Church by E. H. Broadbent. Pickering and Inglis (1931).

Chapter 6 The 1858 Awakening in America

The Flaming Tongue by J. Edwin Orr. Moody Press (1973).

The Second Evangelical Awakening in Britain by J. Edwin Orr. Marshall Morgan & Scott (1949).

The History of Revivals by William E. Allen. Revival Publishing Co. (1951).

The Re-Study of Revival and Revivalism by J. Edwin Orr. Oxford Association for Research in Revival or Evangelical Awakening (1981).

Revival Year Sermons by C. H. Spurgeon. Banner of Truth Trust (1959).

Chapter 7 Ulster 1859

History of Revivals by William E. Allen. Revival Publishing Co. (1951).

The Fervent Prayer by J. Edwin Orr. Moody Press (1974).

The Re-Study of Revival and Revivalism by J. Edwin Orr. Oxford Assoc. for Research in Revival (1981).

Chapter 8 Britain 1859

Evangelicalism in England by E. J. Poole-Connor. Henry E. Walter Ltd (1959).

The Fervent Prayer by J. Edwin Orr. Moody Press (1974).

The Second Evangelical Awakening in Britain by J. Edwin Orr. Marshall Morgan & Scott (1949).

Chapter 9 Wales 1904

Invasion of Wales by the Spirit Through Evan Roberts by James A. Stewart. Christian Literature Crusade (1963).

Pioneers of Revival by Charles Clarke. Fountain Trust (1971).

The Re-Study of Revival and Revivalism by J. Edwin Orr. Oxford Association for Research in Revival (1981).

I Saw the Welsh Revival by David Matthews. Moody Press (1951).

Rent Heavens – The Revival of 1904 by R. B. Jones. Pioneer Mission (1931).

Baker's Dictionary of Practical Theology Edited by Ralph G. Turnbull. Marshall Morgan and Scott (1967).

Chapter 10 The Latin American Explosion

Look out! The Pentecostals are Coming by Peter Wagner. Coverdale House Publishers (1973).

The Flame Still Spreads by David Coombes. Lutterworth Press (1974).

Write the Vision. A Biography of J. Edwin Orr by Bishop A. J. Appasamy. Marshall Morgan and Scott (1964).

Baker's Dictionary of Practical Theology Edited by Ralph G. Turnbull. Marshall Morgan & Scott (1967).

Bright Wind of the Spirit by Steve Durasoff. Logos Int. N. Jersey (1970).

The Flaming Tongue by J. Edwin Orr. Moody Press (1973).

Chapter 11 The Long Arm of Armenian Destiny

The Happiest People On Earth The Personal Story of Demos Shakarian as told to John & Elizabeth Sherrill. Hodder & Stoughton (1975).

Out Of The Ark The Biography of Sisag Manoogian by his daughter, Mrs. Rhoda Carswell, in duplicated form.

Chapter 12 Africa – God's Wind of Change

Dedication Magazine, March/April 1980. Interview with Patrick Johnstone by Wesley Richards. Published by Christian Witness, Slough.

Restoration Magazine, 1978. Interview with Len Moules by Dave Tomlinson. Published by Harvest Time, Bradford.

I Love Idi Amin by Bishop Festo Kivengere. Marshall Morgan & Scott (1977).

Restoration Magazine, 1978. 'Revivals of our times' by Len Moules. Published by Harvest Time, Bradford.

Evangelical Awakenings in Africa by J. Edwin Orr. Bethany Fellowship Inc. (1975).

194

Redemption Tidings Magazine, 28th June 1979. Interview with Reinhard Bonnke by Colin Whittaker. Published by Assemblies of God in Gt. Britain & Ireland.

Redemption Tidings Magazine, 5th November, 1981. Report on Reinhard Bonnke's Birmingham Crusade.

Pentecost Magazine, June/August 1965. Report on Nicholas Bhengu. Published by Donald Gee for the Pentecostal World Conference.

World Pentecost Magazine 3rd Issue 1973. 'Nicholas B. H. Benghu' by the Rev. V. S. Bond. Published by Percy S. Brewster for the Pentecostal World Conference.

Revival Report Issues 1, 2 and 3, 1979; 6/7 and 8/9 1980; 5/6 1981; 2 and 6 1982; 1, 3, 4 and 5 1983. Editor: Ron Steele. Published by Christ For All Nations.

Chapter 13 Indonesia – Revolution and Revival.

World Pentecost Magazine, 1st issue 1973. '50 Years of Pentecost in Indonesia' by the Rev. A. H. Mandey. Published by Percy S. Brewster for the Pentecostal World Conference.

Miracles in Indonesia by Don Granford, Tyndale House Publishers (1972).

Redemption Tidings Magazine, 1st March 1984. Interview with Harvey Walker of Tawangmango Bible School, Indonesia, by Colin Whittaker.

Chapter 14 The Korean Pentecost

The Korean Revival by René Monod. Hodder & Stoughton (1971).

History of the Expansion of Christianity, Vol. 5, by Kenneth S. Latourette. Paternoster Press (1971).

The 20th Century Outside Europe. Harper & Row (1970)

World Pentecost Magazine, December 1964. Article by Dr. R. V. Finlay.

World Pentecost Magazine, March 1984. Article by Linda R. Mervin.

Evangelical Awakenings in Eastern Asia by J. Edwin Orr. Bethany Fellowship Inc. (1975).

Dream Your Way to Success by Nell L. Kennedy. Logos International (1980).

World Pentecost Magazine, Issue 10 Dec 1964–Feb 1965. 'Miracles in Korea' by Dr. Robert V. Finley.

Chrarisma Magazine, June 1982. 'The world's largest pastorate' by Jamie Buckingham. Plus Communication Inc.

Chapter 15 The China Miracle

John Sung — Flame For God In The Far East by Leslie T. Lyall. OMF Books (1954).

China — A New Day by W. Stanley Mooneyham. Logos International (1979).

Redemption Tidings Magazine, 12th January 1984. Report of speech given by Dr. Hudson Taylor III in Toronto 1973.

Australian Evangel 'Mama Kwong – Modern Day China Miracle' by Reginald Klimionok. Reproduced by *Redemption Tidings* 3rd November 1983 and 18th January 1984.

Redemption Tidings Magazine 1st December 1983. Article by Frank Holder.

Evangelical Awakenings in Eastern Asia by J. Edwin Orr. Bethany Fellowship Inc. (1975).

The Flaming Tongue by J. Edwin Orr. Moody Press (1973).

Operation World by P. J. Johnston. STL Publications (1978).

Chapter 16 The Hebrides Revival 1949

Address by Duncan Campbell at Keswick 1952. Duplicated.

God's Answer – Revival Sermons by Duncan Campbell. Faith Mission (1960).

The Re-Study of Revival and Revivalism by J. Edwin Orr. Oxford Assoc. for Research in Revival (1981).

Chapter 17 Why not Revival where I Live?

Lectures on Revivals of Religion by Charles G. Finney. Fleming H. Revel Company (1868). (First published 1835).

God's New Thing by James A. Stewart. Revival Literature, Pa.

Lectures on Revivals by W. B. Sprague. Banner of Truth Trust (1959).

Another Wave Rolls In by Frank Bartleman. Whitaker Books.

The Re-Study of Revival and Revivalism by J. Edwin Orr. Oxford Assoc for Research in Revival (1982).

Chapter 18 What are the Conditions for Revival?

Prayer is Invading the Impossible by Jack W. Hayford. Logos International (1977).

The Pentecostal Movement by Donald Gee. Redemption Tidings Bookroom (1941 Edition).

Mrs. Vonette Bright World Evangelisation Information News. WEIS January 1984.

Invasion of Wales by the Spirit by James A. Stewart. Christian Literature Crusade (1963).

Is a New Wave of Revival Coming? by Ralph Mahoney. World Missionary Assistance Plan (1982).

Gateway Magazine. Winter 1983 Article by the Rev. H. Brash Bonsall. Published by Birmingham Bible Institute.

Redemption Tidings Magazine, 18th June 1981. Interview with Yonggi Cho by Colin Whittaker.

The Flaming Tongue by J. Edwin Orr. Moody Press (1973).

Restoration Magazine, 1978. 'Revivals of our times' by Len Moules.

The Re-Study of Revival and Revivalism by J. Edwin Orr. Oxford Association for Research in Revival (1981).

Charisma Magazine, December 1983. 'Receive or resist?' by James Robinson.

SEVEN GREAT PRAYER WARRIORS
Colin Whittaker

The life stories of seven historical figures whose dedication to prayer was outstanding – Charles Grandison Finney; George Müller; David Brainerd; Madame Güyon; Rees Howell; John 'Praying' Hyde; Hudson Taylor. Their lives of extraordinary faith and perseverance remain an inspiration and encouragement to Christians today.

RICH IN FAITH
Colin Whittaker

The author identifies ten specific ways to keep going on the road to faith-riches, starting where faith must always begin – with God himself. He takes the reader through the gift of new birth, of Christ himself, the Holy Spirit, the Bible, signs and wonders, evangelism, tongues and finally to eternal life with Christ.

THE CROSS AND THE SWITCHBLADE

David Wilkerson

One of the all-time best sellers of Christian paperbacks! An amazing and breathtaking description of one man's adventure in faith into New York gangland. If Christianity can work here it will work anywhere.

No Christian should miss this modern Acts of the Apostles.

ISBN 00233　　　　　**176 pp**　　　　　**Pocket paperback**

Other Marshall Pickering Paperbacks

ISSUES FACING CHRISTIANS TODAY
New revised and updated edition

John Stott

In this major appraisal of contemporary social and moral questions, John Stott defines Christian thought on the complex global, social and sexual issues that confront us and provides a valuable resource for Christians responding to the need to seek the renewal of society.

THE SACRED DIARY OF ADRIAN PLASS AGED 37¾

Illustrated by Dan Donovan

Adrian Plass

A full-length, side-splitting paperback based on the hilarious diary entries in Christian Family magazine of Adrian Plass, 'an amiable but somewhat inept Christian'. By his own confession, Adrian 'makes many mistakes and is easily confused', but a reassuring sense of belonging to the family of God is the solid, underlying theme. Continues to be a best-selling title.

Other Marshall Pickering Titles

HEROES OF THE CROSS

An ever-popular series of short biographies of famous Christians for younger readers. Inspiring and entertaining, they are enjoyed by readers of all ages.

CORRIE

Kathleen White

The story of Corrie ten Boom is one of the most remarkable sagas of Christian heroism. Taken as prisoner by the Nazis for protecting her Jewish friends, her faith sustained her and many others during the war and afterwards.

ISBN 10614   **96 pp**   **Pocket paperback**

MOODY AND SANKEY

David Bennett

The colourful story of the famous evangelistic 'duo' Moody & Sankey, whose work together had an immense impact worldwide. With Moody's dynamic preaching and Sankey's gospel music, thousands were won to the Christian faith and their influence is still bringing people to Christ a century later.

ISBN 18801   **128 pp**   **Pocket paperback**

GEORGE MÜLLER
Children's Champion

Roger Steer

George Müller's pioneering work in child care among the orphans of Bristol has rightly achieved legendary status. His example of total trust in God to meet the needs of ten thousand helpless children is still a shining inspiration.

ISBN 11386   **96pp**   **Pocket paperback**